INTER-RATER RELIABILITY ANALYSIS
USING SAS

Other Books by the author:

▶ HANDBOOK OF INTER-RATER RELIABILITY, (5th Edition)
The Definitive Guide to Measuring the Extent of Agreement Among Multiple Raters
VOLUME 1: Analysis of Categorical Ratings
ISBN: 1792354630 / 978-1792354632

▶ HANDBOOK OF INTER-RATER RELIABILITY, (5th Edition)
The Definitive Guide to Measuring the Extent of Agreement Among Multiple Raters
VOLUME 2: Analysis of Quantitative Ratings
ISBN: 1792354649 / 978-1792354649

▶ Beginner's Guide to Principal Components: Applications with Microsoft Excel
ISBN: 0970806256 / 978-0970806253

https://agreestat.com/books/

INTER-RATER RELIABILITY ANALYSIS USING SAS®

A Practical Guide for Analyzing, Categorical and Quantitative Ratings

Kilem Li Gwet, Ph.D.

AgreeStat Analytics
P.O. Box 2696
Gaithersburg, MD 20886-2696
USA

Published by AgreeStat Analytics. Printed and bound in the United States of America.

AgreeStat Analytics
PO BOX 2696,
Gaithersburg, MD 20886-2696
e-mail: contact@agreestat.com

Publisher's Cataloguing in Publication Data:

Gwet, Kilem Li
Inter-Reliability Analysis using SAS®
A Practical Guide for Analyzing Categorical and Quantitative Ratings/ By Kilem Li Gwet

p. cm.

Includes bibliographical references and index.

1. Biostatistics
2. Statistical Methods
3. Statistics - Study - Learning. I. Title.
ISBN 978-1-7923-7488-3

Preface

I wrote this book, primarily to assist researchers and students with the calculation of various inter-rater reliability coefficients using the **SAS** system. For categorical ratings, you will learn how to use **SAS** for computing various chance-corrected agreement coefficients (CAC) such as Cohen's kappa, Gwet's AC_1/AC_2, Krippendorff's alpha and many others. For quantitative ratings, you will learn how **SAS** can be used to compute different variants of the Intraclass Correlation Coefficient (ICC).

The use of **SAS** in this book is basic. Therefore, you do not need expert-level knowledge of **SAS** to find this book useful. However, I expect you to have some familiarity with the **SAS** environment, to be able to run an existing **SAS** macro and to use function modules included in a **SAS/IML** library. Even if your knowledge of **SAS** is limited, you will still be able to download all the programs discussed in this book, and to follow step-b-step instructions so that you can reproduce the same results. If you do not have access to **SAS** , you may still be able to use the free cloud-based **SAS**® OnDemand for Academics. For this, you may create a **SAS** profile to access this very user-friendly platform using the following link:

$$\text{https://welcome.oda.sas.com/}$$

Whichever version of **SAS** you are using, you will want to ensure that you have access the **IML** software. Some of the solutions recommended in this book require the use of **SAS/IML** functions, as previously mentioned.

This book does not present a rigorous mathematical description of the different inter-rater reliability coefficients discussed. Interested readers may want to see Gwet (2021a, volume 1) for a comprehensive treatment of chance-corrected agreement coefficients to analyze categorical ratings, or Gwet (2021b, volume 2) for a formal treatment of intraclass correlation coefficients used in the analysis of quantitative ratings. The focus of this book is on computational methods with SAS .

For now, FREQ and SURVEYFREQ are the only built-in SAS procedures with limited capability for analyzing categorical ratings. Most practitioners will only need the FREQ procedure for their analysis. Both procedures produce the exact same agreement coefficients. However, if your ratings come from a survey, which is based on a complex sampling design[1], then only SURVEYFREQ will give you valid standard error estimates. SURVEYFREQ accounts for the complexity of the sample to compute the correct standard error whereas FREQ always assumes that all subjects had the same chance of being selected.

For SAS/STAT® version 15.2 or later, these 2 procedures allow you to compute the unweighted and weighted versions of Cohen's kappa as well as the unweighted Gwet's AC_1 and the unweighted Prevalence-Adjusted Bias-Adjusted Kappa coefficient or PABAK. However, the number of raters that can be analyzed is limited to 2 and the 3 agreement coefficients are used to analyze categorical ratings only. Consequently, if you want to analyze multiple raters, use alternative agreement coefficients other than kappa, PABAK and AC_1, or analyze quantitative ratings that require the use of intraclass correlations, then you will need a special SAS macro function or a SAS/IML function module. In this book, I will present SAS macro functions and SAS/IML libraries that you will be able to use to achieve all these goals.

This book is divided into 5 chapters. Chapter 1 provides a general overview of what SAS has to offer in the area of inter-rater reliability analysis. I will point out some advantages as well as some disadvantages for using the FREQ procedure. Chapter 2 describes different approaches for analyzing categorical ratings from a two-rater inter-rater reliability study. In chapter 3, I discuss

---

[1]A complex sampling design involves sample selection schemes such stratification or clustering where some subjects have a higher chance of being selected to participate in a study than others.

various approaches for analyzing categorical ratings from multiple raters. SAS macro functions as well as new SAS/IML libraries of function modules will be presented. Chapter 4 focuses on the analysis of quantitative ratings. I will present a SAS macro and other SAS/IML functions that allow you to compute various intraclass correlations. Finally, chapter 5 will review miscellaneous techniques for analyzing categorical ratings. These techniques include comparing the difference of 2 agreement coefficients for statistical significance or the benchmarking of agreement coefficients to qualify the strength of agreement among raters.

Kilem Li Gwet, Ph.D.

Contents

CHAPTER 1

The SAS Solution and Its Problems

Contents

1.1   Introduction

My book entitled "Handbook of Inter-Rater Reliability: *Volume 1: Chance-corrected Agreement Coefficients for Categorical Ratings*," (see Gwet, 2021a) is essentially about methodology. It discusses the fundamentals of several techniques for evaluating the extent of agreement among raters based on categorical ratings. In this book, I have decided to shift my focus, from presenting the methods to producing numbers. Because the focus is on production, I will confine myself to presenting a non-mathematical review of the techniques where appropriate, and to concentrate on one technology, which is the **SAS** software. **SAS** is a massive and expensive system, which is typically licensed to institutions such as universities, pharmaceutical companies, financial institutions or government agencies. It is therefore assumed that you already know **SAS** and can access it through your institution.

It is worth mentioning that an interesting learning edition of **SAS** known as "SAS OnDemand for Academics" is available for free to everybody. You can use the link https://welcome.oda.sas.com to set up a **SAS** profile and be able to use this learning edition. Setting up a **SAS** profile is a straightforward process. This product is very convenient since it is in the cloud and is therefore accessible with a browser from wherever you have Internet access. Although, **SAS** OnDemand for Academics is limited in terms of the amount of data it can processed, I still use it today to write new programs and test them on small datasets.

Most inter-rater reliability experiments involve small datasets. Therefore, many researchers in the field of inter-rater reliability should be able to process most of their datasets with **SAS** OnDeman for Academics. I like this software and invite you to check it out if you have not yet done so.

To respond to the growing demand from researchers for software products that can compute inter-rater reliability coefficients, particularly Cohen's Kappa (see Cohen, 1960) and Gwet's AC_1 (see Gwet, 2008a), **SAS** now includes options in the FREQ procedure for calculating kappa, its weighted version proposed by Cohen (1968), Gwet's AC_1 as well as the Prevalence-Adjusted Bias-Adjusted Kappa of Byrt et al. (1993). In addition to computing these coefficients, the FREQ procedure also computes the associated precision measures, such as the standard errors, P-values, and confidence intervals. Researchers who already use SAS can now take advantage of these features. However, the solution proposed by SAS with its FREQ procedure is imperfect and may lead to potentially serious problems if not used with caution. It also has some limitations that you must be aware of. These problems and limitations are discussed in sections 1.2 and 1.3. This chapter will attempt to clarify and document many of them, and to propose solutions.

1.2   Limitations of the SAS Solution

There are 2 main limitations associated with the built-in SAS solution to the problem of inter-rater reliability.

- The first limitation is with the number of raters that must equal 2 if you are using the FREQ procedure.

- The second limitation is with the choice of agreement coefficients you want to use. Currently, the FREQ procedure[1] offers 3 agreement coefficients. These coefficients are Cohen's kappa of Cohen (1960), Gwet's AC_1 of Gwet (2008a) and the Prevalence-Adjusted Bias-Adjusted Kappa (PABAK) of Byrt et al. (1993).

  You cannot yet compute Gwet's AC_2 with any weight, nor any weighted PABAK coefficient. PABAK is a special version of the more general Brennan-Prediger coefficient of Brennan and Prediger (1981) , and its weighted version is discussed by Gwet (2021a) . Other agreement coefficients not implemented in the FREQ procedure are Scott's Pi of Scott (1955) or Krippendorff's alpha.

---

[1] I am referring to SAS/STAT version 15.2.

These 2 limitations are further discussed in the next 2 sections.

1.2.1　Number of Raters Limited to 2

The implementation of Kappa in the **FREQ** procedure is almost entirely based on the content of Fleiss et al. $(2003)^2$, and is limited to 2 raters only. Many inter-rater reliability experiments involve 3 raters or more. Although several agreement coefficients have been proposed in the literature for multiple raters and categorical ratings, none is yet implemented in **SAS**. However, the **SAS** Institute's support group has developed the **magree.sas** macro program that could be downloaded using the following link:

https://support.sas.com/kb/25/addl/fusion_25006_12_magree.sas.txt

This macro program is also based entirely on Fleiss et al. (2003) recommendations. However, some of these recommendations, particularly those related to the standard error of Fleiss' generalized kappa are questionable. Gwet (2021c) proposed a more accurate expression for calculating the standard error of Fleiss' generalized kappa coefficient. For categorical ratings, the **magree.sas** macro can compute Fleiss' generalized kappa as well as Gwet's AC_1/AC_2. Alternative solutions for multiple raters including other agreement coefficients such as Conger's kappa (see Conger, 1980) or Krippendorff's alpha (see Krippendorff, 2004) are discussed in chapter 3.

1.2.2　Limited choice of coefficients

As previously mentioned, the **FREQ** procedure of **SAS/STAT**® version 15.2 implements Cohen's kappa, Gwet's AC_1 and PABAK coefficients. The recent

---

[2]This book is actually a revision of Fleiss (1981) that was published by others.

implementation of both PABAK and AC_1 is unquestionably a welcome addition to the host of statistical techniques that can now be handle by the **FREQ** procedure. Since kappa is vulnerable to the paradoxes discussed by Cicchetti and Feinstein (1990) and Feinstein and Cicchetti (1990), having more paradox-resistant alternatives to kappa such as PABAK and AC_1 can only be appreciated. However, a few other agreement coefficients not yet implemented in **SAS** have been proposed and are currently being used when the number of raters is limited to 2. Two such coefficients are Krippendorff's alpha by Krippendorff (1970) and Scott's Pi proposed by Scott (1955). Krippendorff's alpha is mainly used in the field of Content analysis. The use of Scott's Pi is uncommon and its interest lies in that the more popular Fleiss' generalized kappa proposed by Fleiss (1971) reduces to it when the number of raters is 2.

In the case of multiple raters (3 or more), researchers may want to explore alternative generalized coefficients due to Conger (1980), Fleiss (1971), Brennan and Prediger (1981) , Gwet (2008a). **SAS** does not offer any built-in solution for these coefficients for an arbitrarily large number of raters. In chapters 3 I will present several **SAS/IML** function modules that implement all of these agreement coefficients, and a few more, and will show you step by step how they can be used.

1.2.3   *On the weighted kappa*

Agreement coefficients can be weighted when the categorical ratings being analyzed are of ordinal type. The concept of weighting is not used here in pure traditional sense as known in statistical science. Cohen (1968) introduced it as a way to give partial agreement credit to disagreement not deemed too serious. The **FREQ** procedure allows you to compute the weighted kappa coefficient. However, there is no weighted version for the other 2 agreement coefficients (i.e. PABAK and AC_1) implemented in the **FREQ** procedure. Consequently, if you want to compute a weighted PABAK or weighted AC_1 (i.e. AC_2), you will need to use the solutions proposed in chapters 2 and 3.

To compute the weighted kappa, **SAS** offers 2 sets of weights to choose from. These are known as the "linear" weights (or Ciccheti-Allison weights) and the "quadratic weights" (also known as Fleiss-Cohen weights) There are many other options that are documented in Gwet (2021a) . Alternative sets of weights and even custom weights are discussed in chapters 2 and 3 and could be used with the solutions recommended in those same chapters.

The calculation of Cicchetti-Allison, and Fleiss-Cohen weights is done in a way that accounts for the type of data categories are expressed in. That is, if you define the categories as character-type values, then the weights are calculated based on sequential integer values from 1 to the number of categories. However, if your categories are numeric, then these numeric values are automatically used for defining the weights. This implementation gives the user considerable latitude in customizing the weights. Some researchers have contacted me about the availability of software products that would allow them to use their own set of weights. Although you can always use your weights, I do not recommend that approach because of the possible abuses that may result from such anarchy. Instead, I recommend that practitioners use numeric categories and change their values to reflect the way they view the seriousness of some disagreements.

1.3   Pitfalls of the FREQ procedure

Using the **FREQ** procedure for computing agreement coefficients and associated standard errors can be risky if not used with caution. Three main pitfalls that all analysts must know are discussed in this section.

- I refer to the first issue as the *Diagonal Problem* discussed in section 1.3.1. If 2 raters use the same number of categories when rating subjects, then there will be no problem as long as these categories are identical. However, if the set of categories used by rater 1 differs from the set of categories used by rater 2, then the **FREQ** procedure will appear to run normally. However, the results will be false because the resulting contingency table will produce a false diagonal.

- I refer to the second issue as the *Imbalance Problem*, which is discussed in section 1.3.2. This problem occurs when one rater uses more categories than the other, resulting in an unbalanced table that the **FREQ** procedure cannot process. There are possible solutions that I will discuss in chapter 2.

- The third issue is referred to as the *Ordinal Data Problem*, discussed in section 1.3.3. You would worry about this issue only if you plan to compute the weighted kappa coefficient. Otherwise, you may ignore it. The **FREQ** procedure generally sorts categories in ascending order, which could make 2 categories adjacent even if the subjects classified in them have little in common. Raters who classify subjects in them will receive a partial agreement credit that they do not deserve.

1.3.1 *The Diagonal Problem*

The **FREQ** procedure of **SAS** was developed many years before the **AGREE** and **KAPPA** options were added to it. But the addition of these options did not change the general way this procedure looks at a contingency table. To be concrete, let us consider the following contingency table:

At first sight, Table 1.1 resembles any ordinary frequency table showing the distribution of 100 patients by rater and pain level. But the raters had to score the patients on a 4-level scale defined by the 4 categories {No, Mild, Moderate, Severe}. Each rater only used 3 of the 4 levels, with the 3 levels used not being the same. Although the information reported in Table 1.1 is accurate, the diagonal in this case does not represent agreement as we normally expect it in the field of inter-rater reliability. In fact, it is not even a "true" diagonal in the traditional sense where each diagonal cell is associated with the exact same row and column labels. It is a spurious diagonal that the FREQ procedure often treats as a traditional diagonal.

Table 1.1: Distribution of 100 Patients by Rater and Level of Pain

		Rater 1			
		Moderate	No	Severe	Total
	Mild	25	5	7	37
Rater 2	No	6	24	4	34
	Severe	11	1	17	29
	Total	42	30	28	100

The AGREE and KAPPA options of the FREQ procedure however, treat all diagonal elements of Table 1.1 as representing agreement, leading to wrong results. In other words, Table 1.1 is a contingency table, but it is not an agreement table. It is the agreement table that you need in order to compute inter-rater reliability adequately. The correct agreement table associated with Table 1.1 is the following:

Table 1.2: Complete distribution table of 100 patients by rater and pain level

		Rater 1				
		Mild	Moderate	No	Severe	Total
	Mild	0	25	5	7	37
	Moderate	0	0	0	0	0
Rater 2	No	0	6	24	4	34
	Severe	0	11	1	17	29
	Total	0	42	30	28	100

In Table 1.2, all diagonal elements now represent agreement. Therefore,

> *When using the FREQ procedure of SAS for calculating agreement coefficients, you must first built a traditional agreement table, so that the calculations are not based on a contingency table with no valid agreement information about the raters.*

This issue is discussed in great details in chapters 2 and 3, and simple solutions proposed.

1.3.2 *The Imbalance Problem*

Consider Table 1.3 representing the distribution of 100 elderly patients by rater and level of function. Once again, this table is a normal contingency table in a traditional sense. One thing however stands out, which is that rater 1 has used one function scale level more than rater 2. This situation led to an unbalanced table with 3 columns and only 2 rows. Therefore our contingency table does not have a diagonal. With no diagonal, the **FREQ** procedure of **SAS** cannot compute any agreement coefficient.

Table 1.3: Distribution of 100 Patients by Rater & Functional Level

| | **Rater 1** | | | |
	Independent	Assistance	Dependent	**Total**
Independent	25	5	7	37
Rater 2 Dependent	17	25	21	63
Total	42	30	28	100

We have another situation here where the contingency table is not an agreement table. With no diagonal in the table, **SAS** will ignore our request to compute agreement statistics. Most mainstream statistical techniques such as the Chi-square test that have historically been implemented in the **FREQ** procedure can work just fine with any contingency table. Contingency tables that are analyzed in statistics, typically involve 2 variables with different levels, and only the distribution of subjects matters. But the agreement table is a very special contingency table, which must be balanced. I refer to this issue as the *Imbalance Problem*, and will further discuss it in chapters 2, and 3 where I also propose simple solutions for resolving it.

The agreement table based on Table 1.3 data is given by Table 1.4. Now you have a balanced table with identical column and row categories, which are also sorted in the same order. This is an agreement table ready for inter-rater reliability analysis.

Table 1.4: Agreement table of 100 patients by rater & functional level

| | | **Rater 1** | | |
	Independent	Assistance	Dependent	**Total**
Independent	25	5	7	37
Rater 2 Assistance	0	0	0	0
Dependent	17	25	21	63
Total	42	30	28	100

Building a formal Agreement Table before calling the FREQ procedure will resolve both the Diagonal as well as the Imbalance problems.

1.3.3   Ordinal Data Problem

Several authors in the literature have advocated the use weighted agreement coefficients so that disagreements, which are more serious and those which are less serious do not receive the same treatment (see Cohen, 1968). It follows from Table 1.4 that Rater 1 rated 7 patients as being dependent, whereas rater 2 rated the same 7 patients as being independent. Here is a disagreement with obviously far more serious consequences that the one that occurred on the 5 patients that raters 1 and 2 classified into the assistance and independent groups respectively. The more serious disagreements generally receive a smaller weight than the less serious ones.

Unfortunately, **SAS** systematically sorts categories in alphabetical order before the contingency table is analyzed. It means that Table 1.4 data for example will be organized as shown in Table 1.5 below.

Table 1.5: Distribution of 100 patients by rater & ordered functional level

		Rater 1		
	Assistance	Dependent	Independent	**Total**
Assistance	0	0	0	0
Rater 2 Dependent	25	21	17	63
Independent	5	7	25	37
Total	42	30	28	100

Both tables should a priori produce the same results. That is only true if you do not care about the weighted Kappa. If you do, then you will want to know that when computing the weighted Kappa from Table 1.5, **SAS** considers the Assistance-Independent disagreement to be more serious than the Dependent-Independent disagreement by assigning the smallest weight (typically a 0 weight) to the former. It is actually the Dependent-Independent disagreement that must be zero-weighted, as it is the one that should not be given any credit towards agreement. Therefore,

When using the FREQ procedure to compute the weighted kappa coefficient, you must name your ordinal categories so that when they are sorted, the resulting adjacent categories will have more similarity than non-adjacent ones.

CHAPTER 2

Analysis of Categorical Ratings from 2 Raters

Contents

2.1   Overview

For inter-rater reliability experiments based on 2 raters, **SAS** offers 2 procedures with options to compute the unweighted and weighted versions of Cohen's kappa coefficient (Cohen, 1960) as well as the unweighted Gwet's AC_1 of Gwet (2008a) and PABAK of Byrt et al. (1993)[1]. These are the **FREQ** and **SURVEYFREQ** procedures. A fundamental question here is "which of these 2 procedures should you use?" Unless your dataset of ratings comes from a statistical survey based on a complex design where some subjects are randomly selected with different selection probabilities, I would advise you to always use the **FREQ** procedure.

The **SURVEYFREQ** procedure was introduced in **SAS/STAT**® 13.1 to meet the needs of researchers who use statistical surveys based on complex designs. For example, in a typical survey sponsored by the US government, minority groups such as Blacks, Hispanics, Asians and Native Americans are selected with a higher probability to ensure their adequate representation in the sample. To avoid a possible bias due to these differential selection probabilities, a statistical weight assigned to each subject and used in the analysis. Although **FREQ** and **SURVEYFREQ** both compute correct agreement estimates using the WEIGHT statement, only the **SURVEYFREQ** can compute the correct standard error after you specify survey design information. Therefore, if the subjects are selected with varying selection probabilities, then you should use **SURVEYFREQ** . Otherwise, use the regular **FREQ** procedure.

SAS implements the computation of Cohen's Kappa and weighted Kappa statistics as an option in its **FREQ** procedure. However, the number of raters to be analyzed must be limited to 2. The more general scenario involving 3 raters

---

[1]Note that Gwet's AC_1 and PABAK are implemented in the **FREQ** procedure since SAS/STAT® version 14.2. If you are using the free SAS OnDemand for Academics then you should not worry about this since it includes the latest versions of each procedure.

or more cannot be analyzed using the **FREQ** procedure. That is, the many extensions of Kappa proposed by Fleiss (1971), Light (1971), Conger (1980) or Gwet (2008a) are not implemented in **SAS** at the time this book is published. However, a **SAS** program presented in chapter 3 can be used to compute these multiple-rater agreement coefficients.

The **FREQ** procedure of **SAS** has other shortcomings when it comes to computing agreement coefficients and must be used with caution. As indicated in section 1.3 of chapter 1, there are situations, common in practice where the **FREQ** procedure will either fail to produce requested agreement statistics or will produce spurious results. The 3 main problems I discussed are the Diagonal Problem, the Imbalance Problem and the Ordinal Data Problem. I am going to present possible solutions to each of these problems in section 2.3.

The use of weights with agreement coefficients to account for partial agreement is discussed in section 2.4, where I present a general overview of the weighting problem in the context of inter-rater reliability. You will see that the **FREQ** procedure has some limited capability, as it only allows for the weighting of Cohen's kappa. To compute alternative weighted and unweighted agreement coefficients for 2 raters not implemented in the **FREQ** procedure such as Gwet's AC_2, Krippendorff's alpha or Scott's Pi coefficient, you will need to use the **SAS/IML** functions that I developed and which are discussed in section 2.5. Other important issues related to the problem of missing ratings are common in practice, and will only be addressed in section 3.5 of chapter 3.

Section 2.2 shows you how to organize input data for the **FREQ** procedure.

2.2   Organizing Your Data

The input file needed to compute Kappa with the **FREQ** procedure can be organized in 2 ways. It could be a Contingency Table or a data file of Raw

Scores. The contingency table shows the distribution of subjects by rater and by category, whereas the dataset of raw scores shows 2 columns of ratings associated with the 2 raters.

▶ **Contingency Table**

The contingency table in our context is the distribution of subjects by rater and by category as shown in Table 2.1.

Table 2.1: Distribution of 15 subjects by rater and category for the 3 categories a, b, and c.

	Rater 2		
Rater 1	a	b	c
a	5	1	0
b	0	3	2
c	1	1	2

This contingency table is specified in a **SAS** program as shown in Program 2.1 by listing all Table 2.1 cells and associated categories. This **SAS** program will compute Cohen's kappa and a few other statistics shown in Figures 2.1, 2.2 and 2.3. This **SAS** program reads the input dataset containing Table 2.1 information in lines 01 through 12. It is in line 18 that I request the calculation of kappa, AC_1, PABAK and other kappa-related statistics. Line #19 requests some tests of hypothesis for the unweighted and weighted kappa coefficients only.

- The first output of this program is the contingency table of Figure 2.1. The **FREQ** procedure always outputs this table even when agreement coefficients are not calculated due to one of the problems previously discussed. It is essential to carefully check this table for imbalance and for the uniformity of row and column labels. If the row labels are different from column labels, it is a red flag and an indication that your results are likely false.

- The second output shown in Figure 2.2, contains all agreement coefficients implemented in the **FREQ** procedure, their associated standard errors and confidence intervals. The simple kappa[2] and the weighted are always both calculated once you specify the **Agree** option. A weighted kappa would be meaningless for nominal ratings (more on this in section 2.4).

- The third output will primarily be of interest if you want to test the hypothesis that the unweighted or weighted kappa equals 0. Typically, when the p-value (i.e. $Pr > Z$) is smaller than 0.05 then the associated kappa is considered to be statistically significant.

Program 2.1. Basic SAS program for computing the kappa coefficient of a contingency table (*To download this program, use the following link:* https://agreestat.com/books/sas2/chap2/prg2contingency.sas)

```
01   data rfile;
02      input rater1$ rater2$ count;
03   datalines;
04   a a 5
05   a b 1
06   a c 0
07   b a 0
08   b b 3
09   b c 2
10   c a 1
11   c b 1
12   c c 2
13   ;
14   ods pdf file="C:\kgwet\out2x1.pdf" style=Ocean;
15      proc freq data=rfile;
16         weight count;
```

---

[2]I would rather refer to it as the "Unweighted Kappa" as opposed to "Weighted Kappa."

```
17        tables rater1*rater2 /
18             agree(ac1 pabak kappadetails);
19        test agree;
20     run;
21  ods pdf close;
```

The SAS System

The FREQ Procedure

Frequency Percent Row Pct Col Pct	Table of rater1 by rater2			
		rater2		
rater1	a	b	c	Total
a	5 33.33 83.33 83.33	1 6.67 16.67 20.00	0 0.00 0.00 0.00	6 40.00
b	0 0.00 0.00 0.00	3 20.00 60.00 60.00	2 13.33 40.00 50.00	5 33.33
c	1 6.67 25.00 16.67	1 6.67 25.00 20.00	2 13.33 50.00 50.00	4 26.67
Total	6 40.00	5 33.33	4 26.67	15 100.00

Figure 2.1: Distribution of 15 subjects by category

The SAS System

The FREQ Procedure

Statistics for Table of rater1 by rater2

Kappa Statistics				
Statistic	Estimate	Standard Error	95% Confidence	Limits
Simple Kappa	0.4932	0.1797	0.1411	0.8454
Weighted Kappa	0.5408	0.1779	0.1920	0.8896
P-B Adjusted Kappa	0.5000	0.1826	0.1422	0.8578
Chance-Corrected AC1	0.5033	0.1846	0.1416	0.8651

Figure 2.2: Agreement coefficients associated with the ratings of Table 2.1

Kappa Details	
Observed Agreement	0.6667
Chance-Expected Agreement	0.3422
Maximum Kappa	1.0000
B_N Measure	0.4935

Test of H0: Kappa = 0				
Estimate	H0 Std Err	Z	Pr > Z	Pr > |Z|
0.4932	0.1838	2.6830	0.0036	0.0073

Test of H0: Weighted Kappa = 0				
Estimate	H0 Std Err	Z	Pr > Z	Pr > |Z|
0.5408	0.2041	2.6491	0.0040	0.0081

Sample Size = 15

Figure 2.3: Statistical test of the null hypothesis $\kappa = 0$

▶ Raw Scores

Rating data collected from an inter-rater reliability experiment is normally not organized in the form of a contingency table. Instead, that data is often in the form of a list of subjects, and the specific categories into which each rater classified them. Here is an example of raw ratings:

```
Subject Rater 1 Rater 2
   1       A       A
   2       A       A
   3       A       A
   4       A       A
   5       A       A
   6       B       B
   7       B       B
   8       B       B
   9       C       C
  10       C       C
  11       C       A
  12       C       B
  13       B       C
  14       B       C
  15       A       B
```

If the raw scores are all we have, then there is no need to create a contingency table showing the distribution of subjects by rater and category to compute Kappa with the **FREQ** procedure. The raw scores can be supplied to **SAS** as shown in Program 2.2. Both Programs 2.1 and 2.2 produce the same outputs 2.1, 2.2 and 2.3. Note that Program 2.1 requires the use of a **WEIGHT** statement in line #16. This statement is unnecessary in Program 2.2.

Program 2.2. Basic SAS program for computing Cohen's kappa coefficient based on raw scores (*You may download this progran using the following link:* https://agreestat.com/books/sas2/chap2/prog2raw.sas)

```
01  data rfile;
02      input subject rater1$ rater2$;
03      datalines;
04   1 A A
05   2 A A
06   3 A A
07   4 A A
08   5 A A
09   6 B B
10   7 B B
11   8 B B
12   9 C C
13  10 C C
14  11 C A
15  12 C B
16  13 B C
17  14 B C
18  15 A B
19  ;
20  ods pdf file="C:\kgwet\out2x1.pdf" style=Ocean;
21    proc freq data=rfile;
22      tables rater1*rater2 /
23          agree(ac1 pabak kappadetails);
24      test agree;
25    run;
26  ods pdf close;
```

2.3   Solutions to the Diagonal & Imbalance Problems

The Diagonal and Imbalance problems were discussed in sections 1.3.1 and 1.3.2 respectively. The right solution to these problems depends on whether your rating data is in the form of a contingency table (c.f. Program 2.1, or whether it is in the form of a 2-column table of raw scores (c.f. Program 2.2). The description of a contingency table in the data step always contains the "Count" variable, whereas the reading of raw ratings in the data step only requires the use of 2 variables rater1 and rater2. If there is no missing rating in the dataset[3], I recommend transforming any dataset of raw ratings into a contingency table by first running the **FREQ** procedure once to create an output dataset with the Count variable. Consequently, I will propose a single solution to both problems that applies to contingency tables only. I will deal with raw ratings in the next section.

It is common in inter-rater reliability experiments that a legitimate category is not used by one rater, therefore will not appear in the rating dataset at all for that rater. While unused legitimate categories will not impact Cohen's kappa coefficient, they will impact Gwet's AC_1 and the PABAK coefficients. Therefore, it is essential to first describe all legitimate categories in the **FORMAT** procedure.

2.3.1   *Dealing with Unbalanced Contingency Tables*

The small **SAS** Program 2.3 produces the contingency table shown in Figure 2.4 and nothing else. That is, the **FREQ** procedure fails to produce the kappa, AC_1 and PABAK agreement coefficients that you explicitly requested in line #15. This problem stems from the fact that the contingency table of Figure 2.4 has more rows than columns. The **FREQ** procedure requires the contingency to be balanced to work. A natural solution to this is to balance this table by adding a "zero" column to it, which will be associated with category "c." It is the general approach that is implemented by Program 2.4.

---

[3]Missing ratings are usually associated with records having only one rating reported, instead of 2.

Program 2.3. SAS program showing the **FREQ** procedure with an unbalanced rating table (*You may download this program using the following link:* https://agreestat.com/books/sas2/chap2/prg2freq.sas)

```
01   proc datasets library=WORK kill; run; quit;
02   data rfile;
03   input rater1$ rater2$ count;
04       datalines;
05   a a 45
06   a b 1
07   b a 2
08   b b 10
09   c a 3
10   c b 4
11   ;
12   ods pdf file="c:\kgwet\freq_imb.pdf" style=Ocean;
13       proc freq data=rfile;
14           weight count/zeros;
15           tables rater1*rater2/agree(ac1 pabak);
16       run;
17   ods pdf close;
```

The FREQ Procedure

Frequency Percent Row Pct Col Pct	Table of rater1 by rater2		
	rater2		
rater1	*a*	*b*	*Total*
a	45 69.23 97.83 90.00	1 1.54 2.17 6.67	46 70.77
b	2 3.08 16.67 4.00	10 15.38 83.33 66.67	12 18.46
c	3 4.62 42.86 6.00	4 6.15 57.14 26.67	7 10.77
Total	50 76.92	15 23.08	65 100.00

Figure 2.4: Unbalanced contingency table produced by Program 2.3

A critical piece in Program 2.4 is defined by lines #02 through #07. It is in this format procedure that you define all categories that were available to both raters at the time these ratings were being assigned to subjects. This program segment could also be a good place for recoding your ratings if you want to. The categories on the left side are those the raters are expected to use, whereas those on the right side are their new values if any. In the current program, I did not want to do any recoding. Therefore, the categories on the left and on the right sides of the equal sign are identical. Even if a category not used by either rater was available to them, you must define it here.

Lines #08 through #17 are used to read the ratings. Lines #18 through #24 aim at creating a new dataset of ratings that would contain 9 records representing all 9 combinations one can form with 3 categories (i.e. $3 \times 3 = 9$). The new dataset `rfile1` supplements the original data `rfile` as follows:

```
rater1   rater2   count
  a        a        45
  a        b        1
  a        c        .
  b        a        2
  b        b        10
  b        c        .
  c        a        3
  c        b        4
  c        c        .
```

The only issue with this "augmented" dataset of ratings is the presence of records with missing count value. These missing values should actually be 0. Converting the missing to 0 is a task that is accomplished with the `stdize` procedure in line #26. This results in the final complete dataset `rfile2` that can be processed by the **FREQ** procedure. Lines #29 through #33 will complete the analysis and produce the agreement coefficients and associated precision measures. Pay attention to line #31 and the "zeros" option, which is required for the **FREQ** procedure to account for the "zero column" in the contingency table of Figure 2.6.

- The first output of Program 2.3 is the complete dataset of ratings of Figure 2.5. Any use of the **FREQ** procedure based on a complete dataset will always produce a balanced contingency table, which in turn will lead to valid agreement coefficients.

- The second output is the balanced contingency table of Figure 2.6. You can see that the number rows and the number of columns are now equal.

- The third and last output of the program is the table in Figure 2.7, which contains all agreement coefficient estimates requested along with their associated standard errors and 95% confidence intervals.

Program 2.4. SAS program that fixes the diagonal and imbalance problems (*You may download this program using the following link:* https://agreestat.com/books/sas2/chap2/prg2xtab3cats.sas)

```
01   proc datasets library=WORK kill; run; quit;
02   proc format;
03       value $catfmt
04           'a'='a'
05           'b'='b'
06           'c'='c';
07   run;
08   data rfile;
09       input rater1$ rater2$ count;
10   datalines;
11   a a 45
12   a b 1
13   b a 2
14   b b 10
15   c a 3
16   c b 4
17   ;
18   proc summary data=rfile completetypes nway missing;
19       where missing(rater1)=0 and missing(rater2)=0;
20       class rater1 rater2 / preloadfmt;
21       id count;
22       format rater1 rater2 $catfmt.;
23       output out=rfile1(drop=_type_ _freq_);
24       run;
25
26   proc stdize data=rfile1 out=rfile2 reponly missing=0;run;
27
28   ods pdf file="C:\kgwet\out3cats.pdf" style=Ocean;
29     proc print data=rfile2;run;
30     proc freq data=rfile2;
31       weight count/zeros;
32       tables rater1*rater2/agree(ac1 pabak)  plots=none;
33     run;
34   ods pdf close;
```

Note that the solution implemented in Program 2.4 assumes that only 3 categories {a, b, c} were available to both raters. Now, assume that 4 categories {a, b, c, d} were available for use and that category d is never used by either rater. This situation will not affect Cohen's kappa. However, PABAK and Gwet's AC_1 will be affected. How would you modify Program 2.4 to make the **FREQ** procedure accounts for all 4 categories when computing PABAK and Gwet's AC_1? The solution is to replace the first 7 lines of this program with the 8 lines of Program 2.5. If you run the modified program, it will generate the revised input file of Figure 2.9 and the revised contingency Table of Figure 2.10, which has 4 rows as well as 4 columns. This contingency table is the correct table that should be analyzed.

Obs	rater1	rater2	count
1	a	a	45
2	a	b	1
3	a	c	0
4	b	a	2
5	b	b	10
6	b	c	0
7	c	a	3
8	c	b	4
9	c	c	0

Figure 2.5: Complete dataset of ratings created by Program 2.4

The FREQ Procedure

Frequency Percent Row Pct Col Pct	Table of rater1 by rater2			
		rater2		
rater1	a	b	c	Total
a	45 69.23 97.83 90.00	1 1.54 2.17 6.67	0 0.00 0.00 .	46 70.77
b	2 3.08 16.67 4.00	10 15.38 83.33 66.67	0 0.00 0.00 .	12 18.46
c	3 4.62 42.86 6.00	4 6.15 57.14 26.67	0 0.00 0.00 .	7 10.77
Total	50 76.92	15 23.08	0 0.00	65 100.00

Figure 2.6: Balanced contingency table created by Program 2.4

Kappa Statistics				
Statistic	Estimate	Standard Error	95% Confidence	Limits
Simple Kappa	0.6275	0.0911	0.4489	0.8061
Weighted Kappa	0.5967	0.0936	0.4133	0.7800
P-B Adjusted Kappa	0.7692	0.0671	0.6377	0.9008
Chance-Corrected AC1	0.8066	0.0601	0.6888	0.9245

Figure 2.7: Agreement coefficients from Program 2.4

The outcome of the analysis based on the revised file is shown in Figure 2.8. A comparison with Figure 2.7 reveals that while kappa-related statistics (unweighted and weighted in the first 2 rows) remain unchanged, PABAK and AC_1 have changed. Therefore,

> *Whenever you compute PABAK or Gwet's AC_1, always specify all categories available to raters at the time the subjects are being rated. All categories, including those never used in the course of the inter-rater reliability experiment matter.*

Program 2.5. SAS program that fixes the diagonal and imbalance problems with 4 categories

```
01 proc datasets library=WORK kill; run; quit;
02 proc format;
03 value $catfmt
04 'a'='a'
05 'b'='b'
06 'c'='c'
07 'd'='d';
08 run;
```

Kappa Statistics				
Statistic	Estimate	Standard Error	95% Confidence	Limits
Simple Kappa	0.6275	0.0911	0.4489	0.8061
Weighted Kappa	0.5967	0.0936	0.4133	0.7800
P-B Adjusted Kappa	0.7949	0.0597	0.6779	0.9118
Chance-Corrected AC1	0.8219	0.0539	0.7162	0.9276

Figure 2.8: Agreement coefficients from Program 2.5

Obs	rater1	rater2	count
1	a	a	45
2	a	b	1
3	a	c	0
4	a	d	0
5	b	a	2
6	b	b	10
7	b	c	0
8	b	d	0
9	c	a	3
10	c	b	4
11	c	c	0
12	c	d	0
13	d	a	0
14	d	b	0
15	d	c	0
16	d	d	0

Figure 2.9: Complete dataset of ratings created by Program 2.5

The FREQ Procedure

Frequency Percent Row Pct Col Pct	Table of rater1 by rater2				
		rater2			
rater1	a	b	c	d	Total
a	45 69.23 97.83 90.00	1 1.54 2.17 6.67	0 0.00 0.00 .	0 0.00 0.00 .	46 70.77
b	2 3.08 16.67 4.00	10 15.38 83.33 66.67	0 0.00 0.00 .	0 0.00 0.00 .	12 18.46
c	3 4.62 42.86 6.00	4 6.15 57.14 26.67	0 0.00 0.00 .	0 0.00 0.00 .	7 10.77
d	0 0.00 . 0.00	0 0.00 . 0.00	0 0.00 . .	0 0.00 . .	0 0.00
Total	50 76.92	15 23.08	0 0.00	0 0.00	65 100.00

Figure 2.10: Balanced contingency table created by Program 2.5

A systematic use of the FORMAT procedure to define all categories available for the study, will always resolve both the Imbalance and the Diagonal problems.

2.3.2   Dealing with Raw Data

In this section, I assume that your input dataset of ratings is in the form of a 2-column table of raw ratings as shown in Program 2.6. This data is in its original form before any processing and was not summarized in any way. As a result, there is no "Count" variable necessary to read this dataset as in Program 2.4. I still assume that there is no missing rating contained in this dataset. That is, each record has 2 valid ratings.

As previously indicated, agreement coefficients can be computed using this dataset by first creating the associated contingency table before using the approach described in section 2.3.1. This is precisely what Program 2.6 does, and its output is the contingency table of Figure 2.11. This dataset can then be used with Program 2.4 to compute the agreement coefficients.

Program 2.6. SAS program that creates a contingency table from raw ratings (*You may download this program using the following link:* https://agreestat.com/books/sas2/chap2/prg2raw2r.sas)

```
01  data rfile;
02      input rater1$ rater2$;
03  datalines;
04  a a
05  a a
06  a a
07  a a
08  a a
09  a a
10  b b
11  b b
12  b b
13  b b
14  b a
15  c a
16  c a
17  c b
```

```
18  ;
19  ods pdf file="c:\kgwet\out.pdf" style=Ocean;
20      proc freq data=rfile;
21          tables rater1*rater2/out=contab(drop=percent);
22          run;
23      proc print data=contab;run;
24  ods pdf close;
```

Obs	rater1	rater2	COUNT
1	a	a	6
2	b	a	1
3	b	b	4
4	c	a	2
5	c	b	1

Figure 2.11: Contingency table created by Program 2.6

2.3.3 Concluding Remarks

One method often suggested in the literature as a solution to the imbalance and diagonal problems, consists of adding fictitious (or dummy) observations to the input file in such a way that there is at least one subject in each category for each rater. The fictitious data will then be assigned a very small weight so as to reduce their impact on the kappa statistics. More details about this approach can be found in Stein et al. (2005), or in SAS Usage Note 22883, which can be downloaded using the link: http://support.sas.com/kb/22/883.html. This approach requires a manual manipulation of the input dataset in a way that is subjective and potentially error-prone.

A second approach, discussed by Liu and Hays (1999) and implemented in their SAS macro called "%kappa", consists of creating the correct (balanced) two-way contingency table from the input data set prior to computing the kappa statistics. The Liu-Hayes solution amounts to filling empty cells with zeros before computing the kappa statistics. Their paper describing the approach they used can also be downloaded with the following link:

http://www2.sas.com/proceedings/sugi24/Stats/p280-24.pdf

This approach also requires the construction of the complete dataset based on reported ratings. It does not allow you to specify categories that may not have been used by either rater. Another approach that is worth mentioning is due to Crewson (2001). You may download a PDF file of his paper using the following link: http://www2.sas.com/proceedings/sugi26/p194-26.pdf. Crewson's approach consists of using fictitious subjects to create additional records in which all unused categories will be represented. However, legitimate and fictitious subjects will be allocated to 2 different domains. The "Domain" dimension will then be used in the **TABLES** statement of the **FREQ** procedure to perform domain analysis. You will only retain the results associated with the domain of legitimate subjects.

The approach I proposed in this chapter for resolving the Diagonal and Imbalance problems consists of first defining all categories available to the raters, then use them to create a complete contingency table. The complete contingency table will allow you to successfully run the **FREQ** procedure.

2.4 Weighted Agreement Coefficients

The notion of "weight" in the field of inter-rater reliability[4] is different from what it is in the field of statistics in general. However, the **FREQ** procedure gives you the opportunity to use the statistical weight in conjunction with the "agreement weight." The agreement weight is an attribute of a pair of categories (k, l). It takes values between 0 and 1, with 1 representing "perfect agreement" and 0, "total disagreement." The numbers in between are asso-

---

[4]This weight is also refer to as "agreement weight" (see Banerjee et al., 1999)

ciated with various degrees of agreement. The statistical weight on the other hand, is assigned to each individual subject in the sample and is the number of population subjects the sample subject represents. It is an attribute of the subject selection process[5].

Consider an inter-rater reliability experiment that consists of assigning one of the 3 ratings Low, Medium and High to subjects. This rating scale is ordinal since Low is lower than Medium, which in turn is lower than High. Consequently, if 2 raters assign the exact same rating to a subject then they have reached perfect agreement and should receive full credit (generally equal to 1) . However, if the raters assign the Medium and High ratings to a given subject, then some researchers may want to see it as a "partial agreement." This "slight" disagreement would then earn this rating a partial agreement credit (generally between 0 and 1). However, the ratings Low and High will be seen as total disagreement and would receive 0 credit. Therefore, an agreement weight denoted by w_{kl} is an attribute of the pair of categories (k, l) and represents the fraction of the full credit that is assigned to it.

In section 2.4.1, I will show how the **FREQ** procedure is used to produce weighted agreement coefficients and associated standard errors. Section 2.4.2 discusses the limitations of the **FREQ** procedure for computing weighted agreement coefficients, whereas section 2.4.3 explores alternative weighting schemes and shows how to implement them with **SAS** .

2.4.1　*Weighted Kappa with the FREQ Procedure*

The **FREQ** procedure produces the unweighted and weighted kappa each time one of the options **AGREE** or **KAPPA** is used with the **TABLES** statement. Therefore, there is a priori nothing special that you need to do to obtain the weighted kappa coefficient along with the associated standard errors. The weighted kappa coefficient in Figure 2.7 was calculated in Program 2.4 without

---

[5]Note that the use of statistical weight is uncommon in the field of inter-rater reliability.

you having to specifically request it. However, **SAS** offers 2 sets of weights for computing the weighted kappa. First, you have the set of linear weights, also called the Cicchetti-Allison (CA) weights and used by default. Second, you have the set of Quadratic Weights, also known as the Fleiss-Cohen (FC) weights and which you must request.

Program 2.7 computes the weighted kappa and prints out the specific set of linear weights that was used. Running this program will produce the output in Figure 2.12 in addition to the previous outputs in Figures 2.6 and 2.7. Figure 2.12 displays the set of Cicchetti-Allison (or Linear) weights, where all diagonal elements have a weight 1 (for perfect agreement) and off-diagonal elements are either 0.5 when 2 categories are deemed close to deserve partial agreement credit or 0 when 2 categories represent total disagreement.

Note that $w_{ab} = w_{ba} = 0.5$, meaning that classification of a subject into categories a and b by 2 raters is seen as partial agreement. Likewise, $w_{ac} = w_{ca} = 0$, which indicates that both categories a and c are seen as total disagreement. Is that the case? This table must be carefully checked to ensure that it reflects a relationship between categories, which is consistent with subject-matter knowledge. Keep in mind that the **FREQ** procedure systematically sorts all ratings in the input file in ascending order and will create Cichetti-Allison weights following that order. This could potentially lead to the wrong weighted kappa coefficient and its standard error, as could be seen from Program 2.8 and its 2 outputs 2.15 and 2.13.

Program 2.7. Computing the weighted kappa based on Cicchetti-Allison weights, and printout the set of weights used in the calculations. *(You may download this program using the following link:* https://agreestat.com/books/sas2/chap2/prg2xtabwted.sas*)*

```
01  proc datasets library=WORK kill; run; quit;
02  proc format;
03    value $catfmt
04      'a'='a'
05      'b'='b'
```

```
06        'c'='c';
07   run;
08   data rfile;
09     input rater1$ rater2$ count;
10   datalines;
11   a a 45
12   a b 1
13   b a 2
14   b b 10
15   c a 3
16   c b 4
17   ;
18   proc summary data=rfile completetypes nway missing;
19     where missing(rater1)=0 and missing(rater2)=0;
20     class rater1 rater2 / preloadfmt;
21     id count;
22     format rater1 rater2 $catfmt.;
23     output out=rfile1(drop=_type_ _freq_);
24     run;
25   proc stdize data=rfile1 out=rfile2 reponly missing=0;run;
26
27   ods pdf file="c:\kgwet\chap2\OutWtedFC.pdf" style=Ocean;
28     proc print data=rfile2;run;
29     proc freq data=rfile2;
30       weight count/zeros;
31       tables rater1*rater2/agree(ac1 pabak PRINTKWTS)
32                       alpha=0.05 plots=none;
33     run;
34   ods pdf close;
```

Kappa Coefficient Weights			
rater2	a	b	c
a	1.0000	0.5000	0.0000
b	0.5000	1.0000	0.5000
c	0.0000	0.5000	1.0000

Sample Size = 65

Figure 2.12: Cicchetti-Allison Weights from Program 2.7

The weighted kappa coefficient and its standard error produced by Program 2.8 are wrong. Nothing about Table 2.15 would suggest a priori that the weighted kappa might be wrong. But it is. What happened? Look at the kappa coefficient weights of Figure 2.15. It appears that the categories H, L and M are sorted in ascending order and the weight associated with the first 2 categories H and L is 0.5, whereas the weight associated with categories H and M is 0. This is nonsense as categories High and Low cannot represent partial agreement with a weight of 0.5, when High and Medium are seen as total disagreement with a weight of 0.

> *The FREQ procedure always sorts all categories in ascending order, and considers 2 adjacent categories in the sorted set as representing partial agreement. This will likely lead to wrong weighted kappa coefficients and standard errors. The solution is to recode categories so that their scending order becomes meaningful.*

Program 2.9 shows how the weighting problem of Program 2.8 is resolved. In particular, you will see in the FORMAT procedure of lines #02 through #07 that the initial categories recoded as 1L, 2M and 3H. This recoding leads to the "correct" frequency table of Figure 2.16. You can now see the revised weighted kappa and its standard error shown in Figure 2.17.

Program 2.8. Program producing the wrong weighted kappa coefficient based on Cicchetti-Allison weights when the 3 response categories are Low (L), Medium (M) and High (H). *(You may download this program using the following link:* https://agreestat.com/books/sas2/chap2/prg2wtedlmh.sas)

```
01      proc datasets library=WORK kill; run; quit;
02      proc format;
03        value $catfmt
04          'L'='L'
05          'M'='M'
06          'H'='H';
07      run;
08      data rfile;
09        input rater1$ rater2$ count;
10      datalines;
11      L L 45
12      L M 1
13      M L 2
14      M M 10
15      H L 3
16      H M 4
17      ;
18      proc summary data=rfile completetypes nway missing;
19        where missing(rater1)=0 and missing(rater2)=0;
20        class rater1 rater2 / preloadfmt;
21        id count;
22        format rater1 rater2 $catfmt.;
23        output out=rfile1(drop=_type_ _freq_);
24      run;
25
26      proc stdize data=rfile1 out=rfile2 reponly missing=0;title;run;
27
28      ods pdf file="c:\kgwet\chap2\OutWtedLMH.pdf" style=Ocean;
29        proc print data=rfile2;run;
30        proc freq data=rfile2;
31          weight count/zeros;
32          tables rater1*rater2/agree(ac1 pabak PRINTKWTS)
33                 alpha=0.10 plots=none;
34        run;
35      ods pdf close;
```

Kappa Coefficient Weights			
rater2	H	L	M
H	1.0000	0.5000	0.0000
L	0.5000	1.0000	0.5000
M	0.0000	0.5000	1.0000

Figure 2.13: Cicchetti-Allison Weights from Program 2.8

The FREQ Procedure

Frequency Percent Row Pct Col Pct	Table of rater1 by rater2			
		rater2		
rater1	H	L	M	Total
H	0 0.00 0.00 .	3 4.62 42.86 6.00	4 6.15 57.14 26.67	7 10.77
L	0 0.00 0.00 .	45 69.23 97.83 90.00	1 1.54 2.17 6.67	46 70.77
M	0 0.00 0.00 .	2 3.08 16.67 4.00	10 15.38 83.33 66.67	12 18.46
Total	0 0.00	50 76.92	15 23.08	65 100.00

Figure 2.14: Distribution of 65 subjects by rater and category, produced by Program 2.8

Kappa Statistics				
Statistic	Estimate	Standard Error	90% Confidence Limits	
Simple Kappa	0.6275	0.0911	0.4776	0.7774
Weighted Kappa	0.5081	0.1179	0.3141	0.7021
P-B Adjusted Kappa	0.7692	0.0671	0.6588	0.8796
Chance-Corrected AC1	0.8066	0.0601	0.7078	0.9055

Figure 2.15: Unweighted and Weighted kappa coefficients based
Cichetti-Allison weights, produced by Program 2.8

Program 2.9. Computing the correct weighted kappa based on Cicchetti-
Allison weights when the 3 response categories are Low (L), Medium (M) and
High (H). *(You may download this program using the following link:*
https://agreestat.com/books/sas2/chap2/prg2wtedlmh9fx.sas)

```
01    proc datasets library=WORK kill; run; quit;
02    proc format;
03      value $catfmt
04        'L'='1L'
05        'M'='2M'
06        'H'='3H';
07    run;
08    data rfile;
09      input rater1$ rater2$ count;
10    datalines;
11    L L 45
12    L M 1
13    M L 2
14    M M 10
15    H L 3
16    H M 4
17    ;
18    data rfile;set rfile;
19      rater1 = put(rater1,catfmt.);
20      rater2 = put(rater2,catfmt.);
21    run;
22
```

```
23    proc print data=rfile;run;
24
25    proc summary data=rfile completetypes nway missing;
26       where missing(rater1)=0 and missing(rater2)=0;
27       class rater1 rater2 / preloadfmt;
28       id count;
29       format rater1 rater2 $catfmt.;
30       output out=rfile1(drop=_type_ _freq_);
31       run;
32
33    proc stdize data=rfile1 out=rfile2 reponly missing=0;run;
34
35    ods pdf file="c:\kgwet\chap2\OutFixedLMH.pdf" style=Ocean;
36       proc print data=rfile2;run;
37       proc freq data=rfile2;
38          weight count/zeros;
39          tables rater1*rater2/agree(ac1 pabak PRINTKWTS)
40                 alpha=0.10 plots=none;
41       run;
42    ods pdf close;
```

The FREQ Procedure

Frequency Percent Row Pct Col Pct	Table of rater1 by rater2			
	rater2			
rater1	1L	2M	3H	Total
1L	45 69.23 97.83 90.00	1 1.54 2.17 6.67	0 0.00 0.00 .	46 70.77
2M	2 3.08 16.67 4.00	10 15.38 83.33 66.67	0 0.00 0.00 .	12 18.46
3H	3 4.62 42.86 6.00	4 6.15 57.14 26.67	0 0.00 0.00 .	7 10.77
Total	50 76.92	15 23.08	0 0.00	65 100.00

Figure 2.16: Distribution of 65 subjects by rater and category, produced by Program 2.9

Kappa Statistics				
Statistic	Estimate	Standard Error	90% Confidence Limits	
Simple Kappa	0.6275	0.0911	0.4776	0.7774
Weighted Kappa	0.5967	0.0936	0.4428	0.7506
P-B Adjusted Kappa	0.7692	0.0671	0.6588	0.8796
Chance-Corrected AC1	0.8066	0.0601	0.7078	0.9055

Figure 2.17: Unweighted and Weighted kappa coefficients based Cichetti-Allison weights, produced by Program 2.9

Kappa Coefficient Weights			
rater2	1L	2M	3H
1L	1.0000	0.5000	0.0000
2M	0.5000	1.0000	0.5000
3H	0.0000	0.5000	1.0000

Sample Size = 65

Figure 2.18: Cicchetti-Allison Weights from Program 2.9

2.4.2   *Limitations of the FREQ Procedure*

While the **FREQ** procedure produces the weighted kappa coefficient with its standard errors, it does not produce the weighted versions of PABAK or Gwet's AC_1. It is not because these weighted versions do not exist. They do. In fact, Gwet (2021a) discusses the weighted versions of several agreement coefficients commonly used by researchers in the field of inter-rater reliability. Subsequent versions of the **FREQ** procedure will possibly implement some of these weighted agreement coefficients.

Do not associate the term "Weighted Kappa" and the **WEIGHT** statement of the **FREQ** procedure. As briefly mentioned in the beginning of section 2.4, the 2 weight notions are not related. Both unweighted and weighted kappa use the **Count** variable with the WEIGHT statement. It is the statistical weight , which tells you that one subject in the dataset actually represents multiple other unseen subjects. What distinguishes the simple (unweighted) and weighted kappa is the use of Cicchetti-Allison (CA) weights (the default set of weights) in the calculation of the weighted kappa. The CA weight is the agreement weight, which only applies to pairs of categories.

The agreement weight is not assigned to subjects. Instead, it is assigned to each combination of categories that the 2 raters may choose. If A, B, and C are the 3 categories a subject can be classified into, then each of the pairs (A,A), (A,B), (A, C), (B, A), (B,B), (B,C), (C,A), (C,B), and (C,C), must be assigned an agreement weight value, that typically varies from 0 to 1 depending on the "seriousness" of the disagreement. The more serious the disagreement, the lower the weight. The **FREQ** procedure only offers 2 types of agreement weights. In addition to the default Cichetti-Alllison weight (or linear weight), you have the Fleiss-Cohen (FC) weight also known as the quadratic weight. Let us review these 2 weighting schemes:

The Cicchetti-Allison (CA) Weights

The values taken by the **CA** weights depend on the type of ratings, which could be of numeric or character types. It is essential for you to have a good understanding of how **SAS** creates the weights, in order to ensure that weighting is carried out properly. **CA** weights are determined as follows:

▶ *Alphanumeric Ratings*
When the ratings are of character type, then *SAS first sorts them* in ascending order before numbering them sequentially from 1 to the number of categories. In Program 2.9 for example, the sorted categories 1L, 2M, and 3H will respectively be assigned the numbers 1, 2, and 3. The

CA weight associated with the (1L,2M) pair of categories for example is determined as follows:

$$\text{Weight}[1,2] = 1 - \frac{|1-2|}{3-1} = 1 - \frac{|-1|}{2} = 1 - \frac{1}{2} = 1/2 = 0.5,$$

where $|-1|$ is the absolute value of -1, which is 1. Note that the denominator $3-1$ in the above expression is the same for all pairs of categories and represents the difference between the maximum and the minimum values.

The **CA** weights for the dataset of Program 2.9 are shown in Table 2.2

Table 2.2: CA Weights for Program 2.9 Data

	1L	2M	3H
1L	1.0	0.5	0.0
2M	0.5	1.0	0.5
3H	0.0	0.5	0.0

▶ *Numeric Ratings*

When the categories that appear in the **SAS** data step are of numeric type, then **SAS** will use these numbers. Suppose that the raters can assign 3 possible numbers 1.8, 4.3, and 5.6 to subjects. The **CA** weight associated with the pair of scores 4.3 and 5.6 for example is calculated as follows:

$$\text{CA}[4.3, 5.6] = 1 - \frac{|4.3 - 5.6|}{5.6 - 1.8} = 1 - \frac{|-1.3|}{3.8} = 0.6579.$$

The whole set of **CA** weights associated with the set of scores {1.8, 4.3, 5.6} is shown in Table 2.3.

Table 2.3: CA Weights for Scores 1.8, 4.3, and 5.6

	1.8	4.3	5.6
1.8	1.0	0.3421	0.0
4.3	0.3421	1.0	0.6579
5.6	0.0	0.6579	0.0

The Fleiss-Cohen (FC) Weights

The process of calculating FC weights is similar to that used to calculate CA weights. The calculations are performed as follows:

▶ *Alphanumeric Ratings*

When categories are of character type SAS sorts them in ascending order, before numbering them sequentially from 1 to the number of categories. In Program 2.9, the sorted categories 1L, 2M, and 3H will respectively be assigned the numbers 1, 2, and 3. The FC weight associated with the (A,B) pair of categories for example is determined as follows:

$$\text{Weight}[1,2] = 1 - \frac{(1-2)^2}{(3-1)^2} = 1 - \frac{1}{4} = 0.75,$$

The denominator $(3-1)^2 = 4$ in the above expression is the same for all pairs of categories and represents the squared difference between the maximum and the minimum values.

The FC weights associated with the dataset in Program 2.7 are shown in Table 2.4. All diagonal elements equal 1. Off-diagonal elements will take values 0.75 or 0 depending on whether 2 categories are adjacent or not.

Table 2.4: FC Weights for Program 2.9 Data

	a	b	c
a	1.0	0.75	0.0
b	0.75	1.0	0.75
c	0.0	0.75	0.0

▶ *Numeric Ratings*

If categories are of numeric type, then **SAS** will use these numbers. Suppose that the raters can assign 3 possible numbers 1.8, 4.3, and 5.6 to the raters. The **FC** weight associated with the pair of scores 4.3 and 5.6 is calculated as follows:

$$\text{Weight}[4.3, 5.6] = 1 - \frac{(4.3 - 5.6)^2}{(5.6 - 1.8)^2} = 1 - \frac{(-1.3)^2}{(3.8)^2} = 0.8830.$$

The whole set of **FC** weights associated with the scores $\{1.8, 4.3, 5.6\}$ is shown in Table 2.5.

Table 2.5: FC Weights for Scores 1.8, 4.3, and 5.6

	1.8	4.3	5.6
1.8	1.0	0.5672	0.0
4.3	0.5672	1.0	0.8830
5.6	0.0	0.8830	0.0

Meaning of the Weights

CA and FC weights do not necessarily have any practical meaning. You will choose one set of weights based on the extent to which you want to downweight serious disagreements. The **CA** weight associated with the *a-b* disagreement in Program 2.7 is 0.5, while the **FC** weight associated with the same disagreement is 0.75. The choice of one weight over another can be largely subjective, and may be decided by a panel of experts. But using simple unweighted kappa when there is a clear hierarchy among categories could underestimate the extent of agreement among raters.

2.4.3   Alternative Weights

The **FREQ** procedure allows you to compute the weighted kappa coefficient with Cichetti-Allison and Fleiss-Cohen weights only. However, other sets of weights can be used as well. A mathematical description of these weights can be found on the following webpage:

$$https://agreestat.com/books/cac5/weights/$$

A more detailed discussion on these agreement weights can also be found in chapter 4 of Gwet (2021a) where the notion of agreement weighting has been extensively discussed. The following 8 sets of weights can been considered:

- *Identity Weights.*   Identity weights for a 4-item ordinal Likert scale are shown in Table 2.6 and their use produces the unweighted agreement coefficient. That is, the unweighted kappa is equivalent to a weighted kappa that is based on identity weights. All diagonal weights are 1 whereas off-diagonal weights equal 0.

- *Ordinal Weights.*   Ordinal weights are solely based on the sequential numbering of ratings with an ordinal structure. Table 2.7 shows an example of ordinal weights based on a 4-item Likert scale. The sequential numbers representing categories do not have any particular meaning.

- *Linear Weights.* These weights are also known as the Cichetti-Allison weights (see Cicchetti and Allison, 1971), are implemented in **SAS** , and can be used with ordinal, interval or ratio ratings. Table 2.8 shows an example of linear weights for a 4-item Likert scale.

- *Quadratic Weights.* These weights are also known as the Fleiss-Cohen weights (see Fleiss and Cohen, 1973), are implemented in **SAS** , and can be used with ordinal, interval or ratio ratings. Table 2.9 shows an example of linear weights for a 4-item Likert scale.

- *Radical Weights.* This set of weights is a compromise between quadratic weights, which give more credit to partial agreements and linear weights, which give less credit to them. They can be used with ordinal, interval or ratio ratings. Table 2.10 shows an example of linear weights for a 4-item Likert scale.

- *Ratio Weights.* Ratio weights have been used (although in the form of distance functions) by (Krippendorff, 1970, 1978, 2004) and can be used with rating data of ratio type. Note that these weights are larger in the middle of the scale. That is, the partial agreement between categories 1 and 2 receives less credit than the partial agreement between categories 2 and 3, which in turn receive less credit than the partial agreement between categories 3 and 4. In other words, any disagreement in the larger categories is considered less serious. Table 2.11 shows an example of linear weights for a 4-item Likert scale.

- *Circular Weights.* Circular weights have also be used by (Krippendorff, 1970, 1978, 2004) in the form of a metric difference. These weights would be recommended if the rating represents the magnitude of an angle expressed in degrees or in radians. The endpoints in this case are generally considered to be close and expected to be associated with large weights. Table 2.12 shows an example of linear weights for a 4-item Likert scale.

- *Bipolar Weights.* Bipolar weights behave like ratio weights at the center of the scale and like quadratic weights towards the tails. Table 2.13 shows an example of linear weights for a 4-item Likert scale.

To use any of these sets of weights in **SAS** , you will need the **SAS/IML** library of function modules I have developed and which is discussed in section

2.5. These functions even allow you to use your own custom set of weights. There is no clear guidelines in the inter-rater reliability literature that would suggest one set of weights for a given dataset of ratings. The set of weights you need depends on your understanding of the measurement scale being used and the seriousness of the different types of disagreement. You should always specify the specific set of ratings you have decided to use in your analysis, and have a justification for their use.

Table 2.6: Identity Weights

| | Scores | | | |
Scores	1	2	3	4
1	1	0	0	0
2	0	1	0	0
3	0	0	1	0
4	0	0	0	1

Table 2.7: Ordinal Weights

| | Scores | | | |
Scores	1	2	3	4
1	1	0.833	0.5	0
2	0.833	1	0.833	0.5
3	0.5	0.833	1	0.833
4	0	0.5	0.833	1

Table 2.8: Linear Weights

| | Scores | | | |
Scores	1	2	3	4
1	1	0.667	0.333	0
2	0.667	1	0.667	0.333
3	0.333	0.667	1	0.667
4	0	0.333	0.667	1

Table 2.9: Quadratic Weights

| | Scores | | | |
Scores	1	2	3	4
1	1	0.889	0.556	0
2	0.889	1	0.889	0.556
3	0.556	0.889	1	0.889
4	0	0.556	0.889	1

Table 2.10: Radical Weights

Scores	Scores			
	1	2	3	4
1	1	0.423	0.184	0
2	0.423	1	0.423	0.184
3	0.184	0.423	1	0.423
4	0	0.184	0.423	1

Table 2.11: Ratio Weights

Scores	Scores			
	1	2	3	4
1	1	0.691	0.306	0
2	0.691	1	0.889	0.691
3	0.306	0.889	1	0.943
4	0	0.691	0.943	1

Table 2.12: Circular Weights

Scores	Scores			
	1	2	3	4
1	1	0.5	0	0.5
2	0.5	1	0.5	0
3	0	0.5	1	0.5
4	0.5	0	0.5	1

Table 2.13: Bipolar Weights

Scores	Scores			
	1	2	3	4
1	1	0.8	0.5	0
2	0.8	1	0.889	0.5
3	0.5	0.889	1	0.8
4	0	0.5	0.8	1

2.5   Computing Alternative Agreement Coefficients

This section presents a SAS/IML library of functions named `agreecoeff2.sas`, which allows you to compute many agreement coefficients beyond kappa, PABAK and AC_1 that the **FREQ** procedure offers. This library can be downloaded using the following link:

https://agreestat.com/books/sas2/chap2/agreecoeff2.sas

Section 2.5.1 describes the problems this library addresses, whereas section 2.5.2 describes the different function modules available in the library and how to use them.

2.5.1 The Problem

The `agreecoeff2.sas` library of functions aims to overcome the limitations of the **FREQ** procedure with respect to the calculation of agreement coefficients. These functions deal with 2 raters only and assume that both raters rated the exact same number of subjects. That is, your dataset of ratings contains no missing rating. The treatment of missing ratings as well as the computation of agreement coefficients for 3 raters or more are devoted to chapter 3.

With the **SAS/IML** function modules in the `agreecoeff2.sas` library, you will be able to compute the percent agreement coefficient, Cohen's kappa, Scott's Pi (see Scott, 1955)[6], Krippendorff's alpha, Gwet's AC_1, and Brennan-Prediger[7] coefficient. The weighted versions of all of these coefficients can also be computed using any of the weight sets discussed in section 2.4.3. These function modules even allow you to supply your own custom set of weights.

2.5.2 The SAS/IML agreecoeff2.sas Library

The `agreecoeff2.sas` library of functions contains the following 6 functions (the input parameters are defined afterwards):

- `pa2_table(x2Tab,weights=I(ncol(x2Tab)),conflev=0.95,`
  `Npop=10**7);`

---

[6]Note that Scott's Pi coefficient is the 2-rater version of Fleiss' generalized kappa coefficient (see Fleiss, 1971).

[7]What is referred to as PABAK in the **FREQ** procedure and due to the Byrt et al. (1993), is actually the Brennan-Prediger coefficient released more than a decade prior (see Brennan and Prediger, 1981).

This function computes the unweighted and weighted percent agreement for 2 raters.

- `gwet_ac1_table(x2Tab,weights=I(ncol(x2Tab)),conflev=0.95,Npop=10**7);`

  This function computes Gwet's AC_1 and AC_2 coefficients for 2 raters.

- `kappa2_table(x2Tab,weights=I(ncol(x2Tab)),conflev=0.95,Npop=10**7);`

  This function computes unweighted and weighted Cohen's kappa coefficients for 2 raters.

- `krippen2_table(x2Tab,weights=I(ncol(x2Tab)),conflev=0.95,Npop=10**7);`

  This function computes unweighted and weighted Krippendorff's alpha coefficients for 2 raters.

- `scott2_table(x2Tab,weights=I(ncol(x2Tab)),conflev=0.95,Npop=10**7);`

  This function computes unweighted and weighted Scott's Pi coefficients for 2 raters.

- `bp2_table(x2Tab,weights=I(ncol(x2Tab)),conflev=0.95,Npop=10**7);`

  This function computes unweighted and weighted Brennan-Prediger (or PABAK) coefficients for 2 raters.

All these functions take the exact same set of parameters that I will now review.

`x2Tab` is a square matrix representing the distribution of subjects by rater and category. Each cell of this matrix is the count of subjects that both raters classified into the corresponding categories. This is the only mandatory parameter that you need to supply to the functions.

`weights=I(ncol(x2Tab))` is an optional weight parameter containing the set of weights used to produce the weighted agreement coefficient. This parameter is defined in the form of a square matrix such as those of Tables 2.6 through 2.13. Its default value is the set of identity weights leading to the unweighted agreement coefficient. The size of this identity weight is the number of categories available to both raters during the inter-rater reliability experiment and calculated as the number of columns of the input matrix.

`conflev=0.95` is another optional parameter used to specify the confidence level with which confidence intervals will be calculated. Its default value is 0.95 or 95%.

`Npop=10**7` is an optional parameter representing the size of the subject population from which the sample of subjects was selected. Subjects that participate in an inter-rater reliability experiment are generally assumed to have come from a bigger universe of subjects. Knowing the size of that universe may improve the precision of the agreement coefficient. Its default value is the following arbitrarily large number $Npop = 10^7 = 10000000$, which indicates for all practical purposes that its impact on the standard error will be negligible[8].

To show you how these functions can be used in a **SAS** program, I wrote Program 2.10 that produced the results in Figure 2.19. This output table shows you the unweighted estimates and associated precision measures of 6 agreement coefficients. These precision measures are the standard error, the 95% confidence interval and the p-value. The p-value associated with the kappa coefficient is 2.939×10^{-9}, which is very small and indicates that the kappa coefficient is statistically significant.

Note that this data was previously analyzed with the **FREQ** procedure (see Program 2.5) and the results shown in Figure 2.8. However, you will notice that the 95% confidence interval in Figure 2.19 for Cohen's kappa and calculated

---

[8]You can replace `Npop` with any large number provided the ratio of the number of subjects to `Npop` is negligible.

with the `agreecoeff2.sas` library is $(0.44548, 0.80954)$ and slightly different from $(0.4489, 0.8061)$ produced by the **FREQ** procedure. The difference stems from the fact that the **FREQ** procedure uses the Normal distribution to construct the intervals whereas the `agreecoeff2.sas` library uses the Student's T distribution. The discrepancy between both approaches is expected to get smaller and smaller as the number of subjects increases.

Program 2.10. SAS program that computes alternative agreement coefficients from a contingency table, using SAS/IML functions (*Download this program with this link*: https://agreestat.com/books/sas2/chap2/prg2xtabiml.sas)

```
01   proc datasets library=WORK kill; run; quit;
02   proc format;
03       value $catfmt
04       'a'='a'
05       'b'='b'
06       'c'='c'
07       'd'='d';
08   run;
09   data rfile;
10       input rater1$ rater2$ count;
11       datalines;
12   a a 45
13   a b 1
14   b a 2
15   b b 10
16   c a 3
17   c b 4
18   ;
19   proc summary data=rfile completetypes nway missing;
20       where missing(rater1)=0 and missing(rater2)=0;
21       class rater1 rater2 / preloadfmt;
22       id count;
23       format rater1 rater2 $catfmt.;
24       output out=rfile1(drop=_type_ _freq_);
25       run;
26
27   proc stdize data=rfile1 out=rfile2 reponly missing=0;run;
28
29   ods pdf file="c:\kgwet\output.pdf" style=Ocean;
```

```
30        proc print data=rfile2;run;
31        proc freq data=rfile2;
32            weight count/zeros;
33            tables rater1*rater2/agree(ac1 pabak)  plots=none;
34        run;
35        proc iml;
36          %include "c:\kgwet\weights.sas";
37          %include "c:\kgwet\agreecoeff2.sas";
38          use rfile2;read all var{rater1 rater2 count};close;
39          categ_vec = unique_vec(rater1);
40          q = nrow(categ_vec); * Number of categories;
41          xtab = shape(count,q,q);
42          mattrib xtab rowname=categ_vec colname=categ_vec;
43
44          kappa = kappa2_table(xtab);
45          ac1 = gwet_ac1_table(xtab);
46          bp = bp2_table(xtab);
47          kripp = krippen2_table(xtab);
48          scott = scott2_table(xtab);
49          pa = pa2_table(xtab);
50
51          kappa_coeff=kappa$1;kappa_stderr=kappa$2;
52          kappa_ci=kappa$3;kappa_pval=kappa$4;
53
54          ac1_coeff=ac1$1;ac1_stderr=ac1$2;
55          ac1_ci=ac1$3;ac1_pval=ac1$4;
56
57          bp_coeff=bp$1;bp_stderr=bp$2;
58          bp_ci=bp$3;bp_pval=bp$4;
59
60          kripp_coeff=kripp$1;kripp_stderr=kripp$2;
61          kripp_ci=kripp$3;kripp_pval=kripp$4;
62
63          scott_coeff=scott$1;scott_stderr=scott$2;
64          scott_ci=scott$3;scott_pval=scott$4;
65
66          pa_coeff=pa$1;pa_stderr=pa$2;pa_ci=pa$3;pa_pval=pa$4;
67          coeff = kappa_coeff//ac1_coeff//bp_coeff//kripp_coeff
68                      //scott_coeff//pa_coeff;
69          stderr = kappa_stderr//ac1_stderr//bp_stderr//
70                      kripp_stderr//scott_stderr//pa_stderr;
71          ci = kappa_ci//ac1_ci//bp_ci//kripp_ci//scott_ci
72                      //pa_ci;
```

```
73          coeff_names = {"Kappa","AC1","B-P","Krippendorff",
74                          "Scott","Pa"};
75          pval = kappa_pval//ac1_pval//bp_pval//kripp_pval//
76                  scott_pval//pa_pval;
77          print coeff_names[L="Coefficients"] coeff[L="Estimate"]
78                  stderr[L="Standard Error"]
79                  ci[L="Confidence Interval"] pval[L="P-Value"];
80      quit;
81  ods pdf close;
```

Coefficients	Estimate	Standard Error	Confidence Interval	P-Value
Kappa	0.6275072	0.0911176	(0.44548,0.80954)	2.9385E-9
AC1	0.8218934	0.0539371	(0.71414,0.92965)	0
B-P	0.7948718	0.059669	(0.67567,0.91407)	0
Krippendorff	0.6264118	0.0939484	(0.43873,0.8141)	7.1006E-9
Scott	0.6235158	0.0939484	(0.43583,0.8112)	8.0363E-9
Pa	0.8461538	0.0447517	(0.75675,0.93556)	0

Figure 2.19: Calculation of Alternative Agreement coefficients from Program 2.10

CHAPTER 3

Analysis of Categorical Ratings for Multiple Raters

Contents

3.1   Introduction

As mentioned in chapter 2, the **FREQ** procedure of **SAS**® can only compute the extent of agreement among two raters. When the number of raters is three or more, no **SAS** built-in procedure can compute the many extensions of Cohen's kappa that were proposed in the literature. However, one of these generalizations due to Fleiss (1971) can be calculated using a **SAS** macro called "**magree.sas**", and which is offered by **SAS** institute as a courtesy service to interested users. This **SAS** macro can be downloaded using the following link:

`https://support.sas.com/kb/25/addl/fusion_25006_12_magree.sas.txt`

This macro program is well documented[1], and implements Fleiss' generalized kappa, Gwet's AC_1 coefficients as well as their weighted versions using various sets of weights. This **SAS** macro is further discussed in section 3.2.

Note that several other agreement coefficients such as Conger's generalized kappa, Brennan-Prediger coefficient and Krippendorff's alpha and their weighted versions are not implemented in the **MAGREE.SAS** macro. To address these limitations, I developed two **SAS/IML** libraries of functions named **agreecoeff3raw.sas** and **agreecoeff3dist.sas**, which are discussed in section 3.3.

3.2   The MAGREE.SAS SAS Macro

The **MAGREE.SAS** SAS macro is best introduced with the analysis of a dataset of ratings. Consider a simple inter-rater reliability experiment where 4 raters named rater1, rater2, rater3 and rater4 must each classify 10 subjects into one of 5 possible categories labeled as 1, 2, 3, 4, and 5. You have 2 options for organizing the data. The first option is to record the raw data as shown in

---

[1]Interested users may find more information related to this macro using the following link https://support.sas.com/kb/25/006.html

Table 3.1. This format shows each rater and the specific category into which it classified each subject. Its main advantage is to capture all the information related to the experiment. The second option is to organize the data in the form of a distribution of raters by subject and category as shown in Table 3.2. This format has the advantage of giving you a quick view of the way the raters scored the subjects. However, you would not know how a specific rater categorized a given subject unless all 4 agreed by classifying the subject into the exact same category.

Table 3.1: Classification of 10 Subjects by 4 Raters in 5 Categories

Subject	rater1	rater2	rater3	rater4
1	5	5	5	5
2	3	1	3	1
3	5	5	5	5
4	3	1	3	1
5	5	5	4	5
6	1	2	3	3
7	3	1	1	1
8	1	1	1	3
9	3	3	4	4
10	1	3	1	1

My advice is to always have the raw data (Table 3.1) at your disposal whenever possible. Note that Table3.2 alone does not allow you to compute some of the agreement coefficients proposed in the literature and can always be recreated from Table 3.1. Moreover, if you only have Table 3.2 information available, you will not be able to use the **MAGREE.SAS** macro. You will shortly see why it is a problem.

Here are some of the most interesting features of the MAGREE.SAS macro:

- For nominal ratings, the MAGREE.SAS macro can compute the unweighted Fleiss' generalized kappa as well as Gwet's AC_1 coefficient. This macro also has the special feature of computing Kappa statistics conditionally on the response category. That is, for each category, the conditional kappa is computed as a measure of the extent of agreement between raters with respect to that specific category. The methods for computing these conditional kappa coefficients are also discussed by Fleiss (1971).

- For ordinal ratings, the MAGREE.SAS macro can compute the weighted AC_1 coefficient also known as AC_2 Gwet (2021a). However, the weighted version of Fleiss' generalized kappa is not computed.

- For quantitative ratings, **MAGREE.SAS** can compute Kendall's coefficient of concordance (see Siegel and Castellan Jr., 1988) for more on this coefficient.

Table 3.2: Distribution of Raters by Subject and Category

Subject	1	2	3	4	5	Total
1	0	0	0	0	4	4
2	2	0	2	0	0	4
3	0	0	0	0	4	4
4	2	0	2	0	0	4
5	0	0	0	1	3	4
6	1	1	2	0	0	4
7	3	0	1	0	0	4
8	3	0	1	0	0	4
9	0	0	2	2	0	4
10	3	0	1	0	0	4

Program 3.1 shows how you can use the **MAGREE.SAS** macro for analyzing Table 3.1 data. The execution of this program produces the output shown in Figures 3.1, 3.2 and 3.3.

Note that lines #01 through #19 reads Table 3.1 data and reorganize it in the long format. That is, the input dataset **ratings** created by this data step will have 3 columns. The first column is **s** (for subject), the second is **r** (for rater) and the third and last column is labeled **y** and contains the score that rater **r** assigned to subject **s**. For the first 2 subjects, this input datafile is structured as follows:

```
s   r   y
1   1   5
1   2   5
1   3   5
1   4   5
2   1   3
2   2   1
2   3   3
2   4   1
```

Figure 3.1 is simply the distribution of the 4 raters across the 5 categories for each of the 10 subjects. You could see that the row marginal is consistently equal to 4, the total number of raters. This is the case since there is no missing rating, each rater having rated all 10 subjects. Figure 3.2 shows Fleiss' generalized kappa and associated precision measures. While the estimated kappa coefficient of 0.3287 is valid, the same cannot be said for the standard error and the other related statistics.

> *Note that the standard error presented in Figure 3.2 is evaluated under the null hypothesis H_0 that there is no agreement among raters (i.e. inter-rater reliability is 0). As a matter of fact, this standard error can only be used for hypothesis testing and not for constructing confidence intervals.*

The correct standard error of Fleiss' generalized was derived by Gwet (2021c) and is implemented in the SAS/IML libraries `agreecoeff3raw.sas` and `agreecoeff3dist.sas` to be discussed in section 3.3. It is the standard error, which should be used for constructing confidence intervals.

Figure 3.3 shows the AC_1 coefficient along with its precision measures. The first column of this table defines 3 scenarios.

- The first scenario (third row from the table bottom) assumes that the group of raters is fixed and that only the subjects are randomly selected. The resulting analysis only applies to this specific group of raters that produced the ratings, but may be generalized beyond the sample of subjects these ratings were collected from.

- The second scenario (second row from the table bottom) assumes that the group of subjects is fixed and that only the raters are randomly selected from a larger universe of raters. The resulting analysis cannot be generalized beyond participating subjects, but can be generalized to the larger population of raters.

- In the last scenario, both raters and subjects are assumed to have been randomly selected from larger universes. In this case, you would expect the standard error to be larger as the analysis can be generalized to both universes of raters and subjects.

Program 3.1. SAS program that computes Fleiss' generalized kappa and Gwet's AC_1 using the MAGREE.SAS SAS macro (*Download this program with this link*: https://agreestat.com/books/sas2/chap3/prg3magree.sas)

```
01    title "Analysis of data from Fleiss (2003)";
02    data ratings;
03      do s=1 to 10;
04         do r=1 to 4;
05            input y @@;
06            output;
07      end;end;
08      datalines;
09    5 5 5 5
10    3 1 3 1
11    5 5 5 5
```

```
12      3 1 3 1
13      5 5 4 5
14      1 2 3 3
15      3 1 1 1
16      1 1 1 3
17      3 3 4 4
18      1 3 1 1
19      ;
20      proc print data=ratings;
21        where s in (1,2);
22        id s r;
23        title2 'Required form of input data set';
24      run;
25
26      %inc "c:\programs\chap3\magree.sas";
27      ods pdf file="c:\programs\chap3\magreeout.pdf" style=Ocean;
28        %magree(data=ratings,
29              items=s, raters=r, response=y,
30              stat=nominal, options=counts);
31      ods pdf close;
```

To evaluate the extent of agreement among 3 raters or more, some researchers would average all pairwise Kappa coefficients obtained from all pairs of raters with the **FREQ** procedure. This is the approach used by Conger (1980) to extend Cohen's kappa coefficient to 3 raters or more. However, Conger's generalized kappa is not calculated by averaging all pairwise kappa coefficients, which would be rather unwieldy. Instead, it is based on a simple and far more efficient equation, which is discussed by Gwet (2021a). To compute multiple-rater inter-rater reliability coefficients, other authors have used different approaches as well. Researchers can experiment with most agreement coefficients discussed in the literature by using the two **SAS/IML** libraries of functions `agreecoeff3raw.sas` and `agreecoeff3dist.sas` to be discussed in section 3.3.

The MAGREE macro
Rating counts per item

The FREQ Procedure

Frequency	Table of s by y					
			y			
s	1	2	3	4	5	Total
1	0	0	0	0	4	4
2	2	0	2	0	0	4
3	0	0	0	0	4	4
4	2	0	2	0	0	4
5	0	0	0	1	3	4
6	1	1	2	0	0	4
7	3	0	1	0	0	4
8	3	0	1	0	0	4
9	0	0	2	2	0	4
10	3	0	1	0	0	4
Total	14	1	11	3	11	40

Figure 3.1: Distribution of raters by subject and category produced by Program 3.1

The MAGREE macro
Kappa statistics for nominal response

Y	Kappa	Standard Error|H0	Z	Prob>|Z|	Standard Error	Lower Confidence Limit	Upper Confidence Limit
Overall	0.32870	0.077866	4.22140	<.0001	0.11548	0.10238	0.55503

Figure 3.2: Fleiss' generalized kappa and associated standard error, p-value and confidence interval, produced by Program 3.1

The MAGREE macro
Gwet's Agreement Coefficient

Fixed	AC1	Standard Error	Z Value	Pr > |Z|	Lower Confidence Limit	Upper Confidence Limit
Raters	0.41057	0.10790	3.8052	0.0001	0.19909	0.62205
Items	0.41057	0.03355	12.2358	<.0001	0.34480	0.47634
	0.41057	0.11300	3.6335	0.0003	0.18910	0.63204

Figure 3.3: Gwet's AC_1 coefficients and associated standard error, p-value and confidence interval, produced by Program 3.1

3.3 SAS/IML Functions

To address the limitations of the `MAGREE.SAS` SAS macro discussed in section 3.2, I developed SAS/IML libraries of functions. Therefore, you need to have access to the SAS/IML software to use them. If you are using a version of SAS/IML that is older than 14.2, it may be necessary to make some minor changes to these functions to make them work. In particular, each function that I developed returns a list, a structure which was introduced only in version 14.2. However, if you use SAS® OnDemand for Academics then you are using the latest version of the software and our libraries will always work.

The SAS/IML functions discussed in this section are included in 2 files. The first file named `agreecoeff3raw.sas`[2] contains several functions aimed at analyzing datasets of raw ratings organized as shown in Table 3.1. These functions are described in section 3.3.1. The second file called `agreecoeff3dist.sas`[3] and described in section 3.3.2, contains several functions aimed at analyzing

---

[2]You may download it here https://agreestat.com/books/sas2/chap3/agreecoeff3raw.sas
[3]You may download it here https://agreestat.com/books/sas2/chap3/agreecoeff3dist.sas

datasets that are organized ion the form of a distribution of raters by subject and category as shown in Table 3.2.

3.3.1   *Analysis of Raw Ratings*

The library `agreecoeff3raw.sas` contains the following SAS/IML functions you will need to compute the following agreement coefficients:

- Brennan-Prediger coefficient, with function `bp_coeff_raw()`.

- Conger's kappa coefficient, with function `conger_kappa_raw()`.

- Gwet's AC_1 and AC_2 with function `gwet_ac1_raw()`.

- Fleiss' kappa coefficient, with function `fleiss_kappa_raw()`.

- Krippendorff's alpha coefficient, with function `krippen_alpha_raw()`.

- Percent agreement coefficient, with function `pa_coeff_raw()`.

Note that all these functions are defined with the exact same set of parameters, and return an output in the form of a list of 2 vectors. For example, the function `fleiss_kappa_raw()` needed for calculating Fleiss' generalized kappa is defined as follows:

```
start fleiss_kappa_raw(ratings,weights="unweighted",
        categ_labels=,conflev=0.95,Npop=10**7);
```

Let us review each of these parameters:

- `ratings` is the input dataset of raw ratings, and the only mandatory input parameter. Each variable in this dataset represents the ratings produced by each rater. For example, to analyze Table 3.1 data, you would ignore the first column, which identifies the subjects. But you will capture the last 4 columns only.

- `weights` is an optional input parameter whose default value is `"unweighted"`. This default value requests an unweighted analysis. Alternative weighting schemes are available and discussed in section 3.4.

- `categ_labels` is an optional parameter, which you can use to describe all possible categories available to raters during the inter-rater reliability experiment. If omitted, then the function will assume that the categories reported in the input dataset `ratings` constitute a comprehensive list of all categories available to all raters during the experiment. If you suspect that some of the categories available may not have been used by either rater, it would be wise to specify them here.

- `conflev` is the confidence level used to create the confidence interval upper and lower bounds. The default value is 0.95. I advise to always use a value between 0.8 and 0.99.

- `Npop` is the size of the target subject population. It is the universe of subjects from which the sample of subjects is assumed to have been selected from. This parameter can be ignored if this value is unknown. A more detailed discussion of the notion of target population can be found in chapter 6 of Gwet (2021a).

Program 3.2 shows how to use the **SAS/IML** functions described above to compute the agreement coefficients and associated standard errors shown in the output table of Figure 3.5. This program also prints out the input dataset shown in Figure 3.4.

If you run Program 3.2 with Table 3.1 data[4], you will obtain the results shown in Figure 3.6, which you can compare to what was obtained with the `MAGREE.SAS` macro (see Figures 3.2 and 3.3). It follows from this comparison that Fleiss' kappa coefficient is identical. However, the standard error obtained using the **SAS/IML** function `fleiss_kappa_raw()` is 0.1217, which is substantially higher than that of the `MAGREE.SAS` macro based on the null hypothesis.

---

[4]If you are interested, you may download this **SAS** program using the following link: https://agreestat.com/books/sas2/chap3/prg3raw10x4.sas

> *Fleiss' kappa standard error produced by the* `MAGREE.SAS` *macro is invalid and should be avoided.*

As for Gwet's AC_1, the coefficient and its standard error when raters are considered fixed are identical. There is some discrepancy regarding the confidence interval bounds due to the SAS/IML function using the t-distribution and the `MAGREE.SAS` macro using the standard Normal distribution. Note that the SAS/IML functions do not yet implement the conditional standard error when subjects are fixed. Check this book's webpage[5] for future updates.

It is in line **#32** of Program 3.2 that Gwet's AC_1 statistics are calculated. The `gwet_ac1_raw` function returns a list of 2 vectors named `ac_outlst`. The first of these 2 vectors contains the 5 numbers associated with Gwet's AC_1 coefficient shown in Figure 3.5 and can be accessed with the command `ac_outlst$1`. The second of these 2 vectors contains the labels associated with the content of the first vector, and can be accessed with the command `ac_outlst$2`.

Table 3.3 lists all functions in the `agreecoeff3raw.sas` library, along with a description of the 2 vectors `mout` and `mlabels` that are returned in the return list. The row associated with vector `mout` shows the variables used to populate it, whereas the row associated with vector `mlabels` shows the labels attached to vector `mout`'s elements.

Program 3.2. Using SAS/IML functions in `agreecoeff3raw.sas` for performing an unweighted analysis of raw ratings (*You may download this SAS program using the following link*: https://agreestat.com/books/sas2/chap3/prg3raw.sas)

```
01   proc datasets library=WORK kill; run; quit;
02   data ratings;
03       input r1-r4;
04       datalines;
05   1 1 . 1
```

---

[5]Here is the webpage: https://agreestat.com/books/sas2/

```
06  2 2 3 2
07  3 3 3 3
08  3 3 3 3
09  2 2 2 2
10  1 2 3 4
11  4 4 4 4
12  1 1 2 1
13  2 2 2 2
14  . 5 5 5
15  . . 1 1
16  . . 3 .
17  ;
18
19  ods pdf file="c:\kgwet\chap3\cac3uwted.pdf" style=Ocean;
20      title "Unweighted analysis of raw ratings from 4 raters";
21      proc print data=ratings;run;
22      proc iml;
23          %inc "C:\kgwet\chap3\weights.sas";
24          %inc "C:\kgwet\chap3\agreecoeff3raw.sas";
25          use ratings;
26              read all var _NUM_ into mratings[colname=rNames];
27          close ratings;
28
29          pa_outlst = pa_coeff_raw(mratings);
30          cg_outlst = conger_kappa_raw(mratings);
31          fl_outlst = fleiss_kappa_raw(mratings);
32          ac_outlst = gwet_ac1_raw(mratings);
33          bp_outlst = bp_coeff_raw(mratings);
34          kr_outlst = krippen_alpha_raw(mratings);
35
36          out = shape(0,6,5);
37          out[1,] = t(pa_outlst$1);out[2,] = t(cg_outlst$1);
38          out[3,] = t(fl_outlst$1);out[4,] = t(ac_outlst$1);
39          out[5,] = t(bp_outlst$1);out[6,] = t(kr_outlst$1);
40
41          cnames = {"Coeff","Std Err","LCB","UCB","P-Value"};
42          rnames = putc(repeat("",6), "$20.");
43          rnames[1] = pa_outlst$2[1];rnames[2] = cg_outlst$2[1];
44          rnames[3] = fl_outlst$2[1];rnames[4] = ac_outlst$2[1];
45          rnames[5] = bp_outlst$2[1];rnames[6] = kr_outlst$2[1];
46
47          mattrib out r=rnames c=cnames;
48          print out[label=""];
```

```
49        quit;
50   ods pdf close;
```

Obs	r1	r2	r3	r4
1	1	1	.	1
2	2	2	3	2
3	3	3	3	3
4	3	3	3	3
5	2	2	2	2
6	1	2	3	4
7	4	4	4	4
8	1	1	2	1
9	2	2	2	2
10	.	5	5	5
11	.	.	1	1
12	.	.	3	.

Figure 3.4: Distribution of 12 subjects by category, produced by Program 3.2

	Coeff	Std Err	LCB	UCB	P-Value
Percent Agreement	0.8181818	0.12561	0.54172	1	0.0000435
Conger's Kappa	0.76282	0.14917	0.4345	1	0.0003367
Fleiss Kappa	0.7611693	0.15302	0.42438	1	0.0004192
Gwet AC1/AC2	0.7754441	0.14295	0.46081	1	0.0002087
BP Coefficient	0.7727273	0.14472	0.45421	1	0.0002376
Krippendorff Alpha	0.7434211	0.14548	0.42322	1	0.0003386

Figure 3.5: Various unweighted agreement coefficients, associated standard errors, confidence intervals and p-values produced by Program 3.2

	Coeff	Std Err	LCB	UCB	P-Value
Percent Agreement	0.5166667	0.08767	0.31835	0.71498	0.0002309
Conger's Kappa	0.33486	0.11889	0.06591	0.60382	0.0201622
Fleiss Kappa	0.3287037	0.12172	0.05335	0.60406	0.024376
Gwet AC1/AC2	0.4105691	0.1079	0.16649	0.65465	0.0041841
BP Coefficient	0.3958333	0.10958	0.14794	0.64372	0.0056397
Krippendorff Alpha	0.3454861	0.12172	0.07013	0.62084	0.0194565

Figure 3.6: Various unweighted agreement coefficients, associated standard errors, confidence intervals and p-values from the analysis of Table 3.1 data

3.3.2 Analysis of the Distribution of Raters by Subject and Category

The input dataset of ratings used in Program 3.1 is a listing of raw ratings showing the specific category into which each of the 4 raters assigned the 10 subjects. The first output of this program is shown in Figure 3.1 in the form of a table that summarizes how the 4 raters are distributed across categories for each of the 10 subjects. This distribution of raters by category and subject is sometimes the only input dataset of ratings you will have. It cannot be analyzed by the library of functions `agreecoeff3raw.sas` nor by the `MAGREE.SAS` macro. Another library named `agreecoeff3dist.sas` contains the SAS/IML functions needed for such a data file. This library can be downloaded from the following web address:

https://agreestat.com/books/sas2/chap3/agreecoeff3dist.sas

The functions included in the library `agreecoeff3dist.sas` allow you to compute the following agreement coefficients:

- Brennan-Prediger coefficient, with function `bp_coeff_dist()`.
- Gwet's AC_1 and AC_2 with function `gwet_ac1_dist()`.
- Fleiss' kappa coefficient, with function `fleiss_kappa_dist()`.
- Krippendorff's alpha coefficient, with function `krippen_alpha_dist()`.
- Percent agreement coefficient, with function `pa_coeff_dist()`.

These functions are all defined with the exact same set of parameters, and return a list of 2 vectors. For example, the function `fleiss_kappa_raw()` needed for Fleiss' generalized kappa is defined as follows:

```
start fleiss_kappa_dist(ratings,weights="unweighted",
        conflev=0.95,Npop=10**7);
```

All these input parameters are defined as in section 3.3.1. Note that there is no input parameter for describing all categories that were available to raters during the reliability experiment. Such a parameter is not needed because you can always include all categories of interest in the input dataset of ratings. Each function returns a list of 2 vectors. The first vector named `mout` contains the coefficient's 5 statistics shown in Figure 3.7. The second vector named `mlabels` contains the labels associated with each element of vector `mout`. Table 3.4 describes these 2 vectors for each of the functions in the `agreecoeff3dist.sas` library.

You will note that Conger's generalized is not listed among the coefficients you can compute with the library of functions `agreecoeff3dist.sas`. It is because, Conger's kappa requires the availability of raw ratings. That is, you need to know the specific category into which a given rater has classified each subject. That information is not available when you only know how many raters classified a given subject into a specific category.

Program 3.3 shows you how the functions contained in the library of function modules `agreecoeff3dist.sas` use the distribution of raters by category and subject to compute the agreement coefficients shown in Figure 3.7. The first output of this program is the input dataset shown in Figure 3.8. Note that all statistics you see in Figure 3.7 are computed in lines #34 through #38 of Program 3.3. The call to function `fleiss_kappa_dist(mratings)` for example returns the list `fl_outlst` and the vector containing Fleiss' kappa statistics can be accessed using the command `fl_outlst$1` as seen in line #41. If you need the labels associated with this vector, then you may use the command `fl_outlst$2` as in line #48.

Program 3.3. Using SAS/IML functions in `agreecoeff3dist.sas` for analyzing the distribution of raters (*Interested readers may download this program using the following link*: https://agreestat.com/books/sas2/chap3/prg3dist.sas)

```
01   proc datasets library=WORK kill; run; quit;
02   data ratings;
03       input subject depression pdisorder
04               schizophrenia neurosis other;
05       datalines;
06   1 0 0 0 6 0
07   2 0 3 0 0 3
08   3 0 1 4 0 1
09   4 0 0 0 0 6
10   5 0 3 0 3 0
11   6 2 0 4 0 0
12   7 0 0 4 0 2
13   8 2 0 3 1 0
14   9 2 0 0 4 0
```

```
15   10 0 0 0 0 6
16   11 1 0 0 5 0
17   12 1 1 0 4 0
18   13 0 3 3 0 0
19   14 1 0 0 5 0
20   15 0 2 0 3 1
21   ;
22
23   ods pdf file="c:\kgwet\chap3\cac3uwted_dist.pdf" style=Ocean;
24       title "Analysis of the distribution of raters";
25       proc print data=ratings;run;
26       proc iml;
27           %inc "C:\kgwet\chap3\weights.sas";
28           %inc "C:\kgwet\chap3\agree_coeff3_dist.sas";
29           use ratings;
30               read all var{depression pdisorder schizophrenia
31                   neurosis other} into mratings[colname=rNames];
32           close ratings;
33
34           pa_outlst = pa_coeff_dist(mratings);
35           fl_outlst = fleiss_kappa_dist(mratings);
36           ac_outlst = gwet_ac1_dist(mratings);
37           bp_outlst = bp_coeff_dist(mratings);
38           kr_outlst = krippen_alpha_dist(mratings);
39
40           out = shape(0,5,5);
41           out[1,] = t(pa_outlst$1);out[2,] = t(fl_outlst$1);
42           out[3,] = t(ac_outlst$1);out[4,] = t(bp_outlst$1);
43           out[5,] = t(kr_outlst$1);
44
45           cnames = {"Coeff","Std Err","LCB","UCB","P-Value"};
46           rnames = putc(repeat("",5), "$20.");
47           rnames[1] = pa_outlst$2[1];
48           rnames[2] = fl_outlst$2[1];rnames[3] = ac_outlst$2[1];
49           rnames[4] = bp_outlst$2[1];rnames[5] = kr_outlst$2[1];
50
51           mattrib out r=rnames c=cnames;
52           print out[label=""];
53       quit;
54   ods pdf close;
```

	Coeff	Std Err	LCB	UCB	P-Value
Percent Agreement	0.5511111	0.0664971	0.40849	0.69373	9.0545E-7
Fleiss Kappa	0.4139265	0.0811928	0.23979	0.58807	0.0001623
Gwet AC1/AC2	0.4448007	0.0841875	0.26424	0.62536	0.0001156
BP Coefficient	0.4388889	0.0831214	0.26061	0.61717	0.0001163
Krippendorff's Alpha	0.4204384	0.0824322	0.24364	0.59724	0.0001616

Figure 3.7: Various unweighted agreement coefficients, associated standard errors, confidence intervals and p-values produced by Program 3.3

Obs	subject	depression	pdisorder	schizophrenia	neurosis	other
1	1	0	0	0	6	0
2	2	0	3	0	0	3
3	3	0	1	4	0	1
4	4	0	0	0	0	6
5	5	0	3	0	3	0
6	6	2	0	4	0	0
7	7	0	0	4	0	2
8	8	2	0	3	1	0
9	9	2	0	0	4	0
10	10	0	0	0	0	6
11	11	1	0	0	5	0
12	12	1	1	0	4	0
13	13	0	3	3	0	0
14	14	1	0	0	5	0
15	15	0	2	0	3	1

Figure 3.8: Distribution of 15 subjects by category, produced by Program 3.3

3.4   Weighted Agreement Coefficients

This section shows you how you can use the two SAS/IML libraries of function modules `agreecoeff3raw.sas` and `agreecoeff3dist.sas` for computing various weighted agreement coefficients for 2, 3 or more raters. Section 3.4.1 reviews the different sets of weights and the general approach for using them, whereas in section 3.4.2, you will see how SAS/IML functions are used in a SAS program to perform a weighted analysis.

3.4.1   *Introduction*

As mentioned in sections 3.3.1 and 3.3.2, almost all SAS/IML functions needed for computing weighted and unweighted agreement coefficients are defined as follows:

- For Fleiss' generalized kappa based on raw ratings for example,

```
start fleiss_kappa_raw(ratings,weights="unweighted",
     categ_labels=,conflev=0.95,Npop=10**7);
```

- For Fleiss' generalized kappa based on the distribution of raters,

```
start fleiss_kappa_dist(ratings,weights="unweighted",
     conflev=0.95,Npop=10**7);
```

With raw ratings, the unweighted Fleiss' generalized kappa is obtained by using the simple command `fleiss = fleiss_kappa_raw(ratings)`, whereas its weighted version based on quadratic weights requires that you specify the `weights` parameter by modifying the previous command as follows:
`fleiss = fleiss_kappa_raw(ratings,"quadratic")`.

With the input dataset in the form of the distribution of raters, the un-weighted Fleiss' generalized kappa is obtained with the command `fleiss = fleiss_kappa_dist(ratings)`, whereas its weighted version based on quadratic weights requires that you specify the `weights` parameter as follows: `fleiss = fleiss_kappa_raw(ratings,"quadratic")`.

When conducting a weighted analysis, the `weights` parameter can take the following values:

- `"quadratic"`
- `"ordinal"`
- `"linear"`
- `"radical"`
- `"ratio"`
- `"circular"`
- `"bipolar"`

A detailed definition of the each of these weights can be found at the following web address:

https://agreestat.com/books/cac5/weights/

> *Note that you may supply a numeric square matrix containing your own customized weights to the* `weights` *parameter. The dimension of this square matrix must equal the number of categories. Otherwise, your SAS program will produce an error message.*

3.4.2   SAS/IML Functions

Program 3.4 analyzes the same dataset as program 3.2 with the exception that this time all agreement coefficients are weighted using the set of ordinal weights defined in the previous section. These weighted agreement coefficients are all calculated in the segment of the program that goes from line #30 through line #35. The results are shown in Figure 3.9, where you can see the weighted coefficients, their precision measures and the set of weights used.

Program 3.4. Using SAS/IML functions in `agreecoeff3raw.sas` for computing weighted agreement coefficients based on ordinal weights (*Program can be downloaded at* https://agreestat.com/books/sas2/chap3/prg3wted.sas)

```
01  proc datasets library=WORK kill; run; quit;
02  data ratings;
03    input r1-r4;
04  datalines;
05  1 1 . 1
06  2 2 3 2
07  3 3 3 3
08  3 3 3 3
09  2 2 2 2
10  1 2 3 4
11  4 4 4 4
12  1 1 2 1
13  2 2 2 2
14  . 5 5 5
15  . . 1 1
16  . . 3 .
17  ;
18
19  ods pdf file="c:\kgwet\cac3wted-ordinal.pdf" style=Ocean;
20
21    title "Weighted Analysis with Ordinal Weights";
22    proc print data=ratings;run;
23    proc iml;
24      %inc "C:\kgwet\chap3\weights.sas";
```

```
25        %inc "C:\kgwet\chap3\agreecoeff3raw.sas";
26        use ratings;
27          read all var _NUM_ into mratings[colname=rNames];
28        close ratings;
29
30        pa_outlst = pa_coeff_raw(mratings,"ordinal");
31        cg_outlst = conger_kappa_raw(mratings,"ordinal");
32        fl_outlst = fleiss_kappa_raw(mratings,"ordinal");
33        ac_outlst = gwet_ac1_raw(mratings,"ordinal");
34        bp_outlst = bp_coeff_raw(mratings,"ordinal");
35        kr_outlst = krippen_alpha_raw(mratings,"ordinal");
36
37        out = shape(0,6,5);
38        out[1,] = t(pa_outlst$1);out[2,] = t(cg_outlst$1);
39        out[3,] = t(fl_outlst$1);out[4,] = t(ac_outlst$1);
40        out[5,] = t(bp_outlst$1);out[6,] = t(kr_outlst$1);
41
42        cnames = {"Coeff","Std Err","LCB","UCB","P-Value"};
43        rnames = putc(repeat("",6), "$20.");
44        rnames[1] = pa_outlst$2[1];rnames[2] = cg_outlst$2[1];
45        rnames[3] = fl_outlst$2[1];rnames[4] = ac_outlst$2[1];
46        rnames[5] = bp_outlst$2[1];rnames[6] = kr_outlst$2[1];
47
48        mattrib out r=rnames c=cnames;
49        print out[label=""];
50
51        wmat = weight_mat("ordinal",t(1:3));
52        print wmat[label="Ordinal Weights"];
53      quit;
54   ods pdf close;
```

	Coeff	Std Err	LCB	UCB	P-Value
Percent Agreement	0.9681818	0.09086	0.76821	1	3.904E-7
Conger's Kappa	0.84366	0.1441	0.5265	1	0.0001101
Fleiss Kappa	0.8502062	0.14704	0.52658	1	0.0001224
Gwet AC1/AC2	0.8989398	0.1069	0.66365	1	4.0539E-6
BP Coefficient	0.8863636	0.11391	0.63566	1	8.491E-6
Krippendorff Alpha	0.833638	0.13099	0.54534	1	0.0000534

Ordinal Weights				
1	0.9	0.7	0.4	0
0.9	1	0.9	0.7	0.4
0.7	0.9	1	0.9	0.7
0.4	0.7	0.9	1	0.9
0	0.4	0.7	0.9	1

Figure 3.9: Weighted agreement coefficients, their standard errors, confidence intervals and p-values from Program 3.4 using "Ordinal" weights.

3.5   Handling Missing Ratings with the FREQ Procedure

Your set of ratings may contain missing values if one rater scores a subject and the other does not. The **FREQ** procedure of **SAS** will handle missing ratings poorly no matter which options are specified. If the **MISSING** option is used with the **TABLES** statement then **SAS** will treat the missing rating as a legitimate category and will evaluate agreement accordingly. If the **MISSING** option is omitted then all subjects associated with missing ratings will be excluded from the analysis. In both cases, the handling of missing ratings by **SAS** is not consistent with the way researchers typically want then handled.

Researchers want none of the data they collect to be wasted. Although only subjects rated by 2 raters or more can be used for calculating the percent agreement p_a, raters rated by a single rater can still be used for computing marginal probabilities needed in the calculation of Cohen's kappa, Fleiss' kappa and many other agreement coefficients. Therefore, all subjects including those for which a single rating was reported, can be used in the calculation of agreement coefficients. However, the FREQ procedure cannot handle subjects with missing ratings according to these guidelines.

3.5.1   The Problem

Program 3.5 produces the 2 tables in Figures 3.10 and 3.11, while Program 3.6 produces the 2 tables in Figures 3.13 and 3.12. It follows from Figure 3.10 that when the MISSING option is used, the "missing" category is treated as a legitimate category and used to obtain an unweighted kappa of 0.534 for a standard error of 0.1787. Figure 3.13 on the other hand, shows that when the MISSING option is not used, the two subjects with missing ratings are excluded from the analysis altogether, which leads to an unweighted kappa of 0.697 for a standard error of 0.1901.

There is a reason why excluding subjects with missing ratings altogether from the analysis is a bad idea. Kappa is based on the percent agreement, and on marginal percentages. While subjects with missing ratings must be removed for the purpose of computing the percent agreement, they must be used for the purpose of computing marginal percentages. These marginal percentages will be based on a larger number of subjects, and will therefore be more accurate. The same reasoning applies to Gwet's AC_1 as well, as the percent chance agreement can use all subjects for which any data was reported. In section 3.5.2, I will show how the library of function modules `agreecoeff3raw.sas` can be used to adequately implement the treatment of missing ratings.

Program 3.5. Using the MISSING option in the TABLES Statement to handle missing ratings (*You may download this program using the following link:* https://agreestat.com/books/sas2/chap3/prg3missfreq.sas)

```
01  data rfile;
02     infile datalines missover;
03     input rater1$ rater2$;
04  datalines;
05  A A
06  A A
07  A A
08  B B
09  B B
10  C C
11  C C
12  C A
13  C .
14  B B
15  . C
16  A B
17  ;
18  ods pdf file="C:\kgwet\out2x3.pdf" style=Ocean;
19  proc freq data = rfile;
20     tables rater1*rater2 /
21              missing agree(ac1 pabak kappadetails);
22     test agree;
23     run;
24  ods pdf close;
```

Program 3.6. Using the TABLES statement without the MISSING option

```
18  ods pdf file="C:\kgwet\out2x4.pdf" style=Ocean;
19  proc freq data = rfile;
20     tables rater1*rater2 /
21            agree(ac1 pabak kappadetails);
22     test agree;
23     run;
24  ods pdf close;
```

The SAS System

The FREQ Procedure

Frequency Percent Row Pct Col Pct	Table of rater1 by rater2				
	rater2				
rater1		A	B	C	Total
	0 0.00 0.00 0.00	0 0.00 0.00 0.00	0 0.00 0.00 0.00	1 8.33 100.00 33.33	1 8.33
A	0 0.00 0.00 0.00	3 25.00 75.00 75.00	1 8.33 25.00 25.00	0 0.00 0.00 0.00	4 33.33
B	0 0.00 0.00 0.00	0 0.00 0.00 0.00	3 25.00 100.00 75.00	0 0.00 0.00 0.00	3 25.00
C	1 8.33 25.00 100.00	1 8.33 25.00 25.00	0 0.00 0.00 0.00	2 16.67 50.00 66.67	4 33.33
Total	1 8.33	4 33.33	4 33.33	3 25.00	12 100.00

Figure 3.10: Distribution of 12 subjects by category, produced by Program 3.5

The SAS System

The FREQ Procedure

Statistics for Table of rater1 by rater2

Kappa Statistics				
Statistic	*Estimate*	*Standard Error*	*95% Confidence Limits*	
Simple Kappa	0.5340	0.1787	0.1837	0.8843
Weighted Kappa	0.2895	0.2527	-0.2058	0.7847
P-B Adjusted Kappa	0.5556	0.1814	0.1999	0.9112
Chance-Corrected AC1	0.5630	0.1814	0.2073	0.9186

Figure 3.11:   Agreement coefficients calculated with Program 3.5

Kappa Statistics				
Statistic	*Estimate*	*Standard Error*	*95% Confidence Limits*	
Simple Kappa	0.6970	0.1901	0.3244	1.0000
Weighted Kappa	0.6512	0.2294	0.2015	1.0000
P-B Adjusted Kappa	0.7000	0.1897	0.3281	1.0000
Chance-Corrected AC1	0.7026	0.1879	0.3343	1.0000

Figure 3.12:   Agreement coefficients calculated with Program 3.6

The SAS System

The FREQ Procedure

Frequency Percent Row Pct Col Pct	Table of rater1 by rater2			
		rater2		
rater1	A	B	C	Total
A	3 30.00 75.00 75.00	1 10.00 25.00 25.00	0 0.00 0.00 0.00	4 40.00
B	0 0.00 0.00 0.00	3 30.00 100.00 75.00	0 0.00 0.00 0.00	3 30.00
C	1 10.00 33.33 25.00	0 0.00 0.00 0.00	2 20.00 66.67 100.00	3 30.00
Total	4 40.00	4 40.00	2 20.00	10 100.00
Frequency Missing = 2				

Figure 3.13: Distribution of 12 subjects by category, produced by Program 3.6

3.5.2   The SAS/IML Functions

Whether you are dealing 2 raters or more, the SAS/IML library of functions `agreecoeff3raw.sas` presented in section 3.3.1 will adequately handle the missing values. However, these functions require that you provide raw ratings. Input datasets in the form of a contingency tables will not work. Your input dataset must show the category into which each rater classified the subjects. A missing rating will occur if a rater does not rate a particular subject.

Program 3.7 shows how the same dataset of ratings used in Program 3.5, produced by 2 raters and containing missing ratings can be adequately analyzed using the SAS/IML library `agreecoeff3raw.sas`. Although Program 3.7 produces the unweighted agreement coefficients shown in Figure 3.14, the inclusion of the `weights.sas` library of functions in line #25 is still necessary. It is because the library `agreecoeff3raw.sas` handles all agreement coefficients as weighted coefficients where unweighted coefficients are seen as have been weighted with identity weights (c.f. section 2.4.3 for more details on various weighting schemes).

You can now compare the results of Figure 3.14 based on an adequate treatment of missing values to those of Figures 3.11 (missing values treated as valid categories) and 3.12 (missing values deleted). Agreement coefficients are all very low when missing values are treated as valid categories. There is no practical reason to use this option unless a missing value is deliberately chosen by some raters for reasons that are understood. Comparing Figures 3.12 and 3.14 is more interesting.

- When library `agreecoeff3raw.sas` is used with 2 raters only, Conger's Kappa reduces to Cohen's kappa. Therefore, Conger's kappa in Figure 3.14 is estimated to be 0.7012 with a standard error of 0.217. For comparison, when you delete all missing ratings, unweighted kappa becomes 0.697 with a standard error of 0.19 (c.f. Figure 3.12).

- B-P Adjusted Kappa is also known the BP Coefficient where BP stands for Brennan-Prediger (see Brennan and Prediger, 1981). The presence of missing values does not affect the magnitude of this coefficient. This is due to missing values being excluded from the calculation of the percent agreement and to the percent chance agreement for this particular coefficient being solely dependent on the number of categories. The standard errors are slightly different mainly due to functions in library `agreecoeff3raw.sas` using all subjects for calculating the standard error including those for which a single rating was reported (see Gwet, 2021a).

- Gwet's AC_1 coefficient and its standard error are also slightly different.

Note that when the number of missing values is limited, then the difference between the different treatment methods is small. The problem becomes more serious when missing values are reported on 50% or more of all subjects in a multiple-rater inter-rater reliability experiment.

Program 3.7. Calculating several agreement coefficients based on 2 raters with missing ratings (*You may download this program using the following link:* https://agreestat.com/books/sas2/chap3/prg3miss2raters.sas)

```
01   data rfile;
02      infile datalines missover;
03      INPUT rater1$ rater2$;
04   datalines;
05   A A
06   A A
07   A A
08   B B
09   B B
10   C C
11   C C
12   C A
13   C .
14   B B
15   . C
16   A B
17   ;
18   proc print data=rfile;run;
19
20   ods pdf file="c:\kgwet\chap3\2raters_miss.pdf" style=Ocean;
21     proc freq data = rfile;
22       tables rater1*rater2/agree(ac1 pabak) plots=none;
23     run;
24     proc iml;
25       %inc "c:\kgwet\chap3\weights.sas";
26       %inc "c:\kgwet\chap3\agreecoeff3raw.sas";
27       use rfile;
28         read all var _CHAR_ into mratings[colname=CharNames];
29       close rfile;
30       print mratings;
31
```

```
32          pa_outlst = pa_coeff_raw(mratings);
33          cg_outlst = conger_kappa_raw(mratings);
34          fl_outlst = fleiss_kappa_raw(mratings);
35          ac_outlst = gwet_ac1_raw(mratings);
36          bp_outlst = bp_coeff_raw(mratings);
37          kr_outlst = krippen_alpha_raw(mratings);
38
39          out = shape(0,6,5);
40          out[1,] = t(pa_outlst$1);out[2,] = t(cg_outlst$1);
41          out[3,] = t(fl_outlst$1);out[4,] = t(ac_outlst$1);
42          out[5,] = t(bp_outlst$1);out[6,] = t(kr_outlst$1);
43
44          cnames = {"Coeff","Std Err","LCB","UCB","P-Value"};
45          rnames = putc(repeat("",6), "$20.");
46          rnames[1] = pa_outlst$2[1];rnames[2] = cg_outlst$2[1];
47          rnames[3] = fl_outlst$2[1];rnames[4] = ac_outlst$2[1];
48          rnames[5] = bp_outlst$2[1];rnames[6] = kr_outlst$2[1];
49
50          mattrib out r=rnames c=cnames;
51          print out[label=""];
52      ods pdf close;
```

	Coeff	Std Err	LCB	UCB	P-Value
Percent Agreement	0.8	0.17056	0.4246	1	0.0006603
Conger's Kappa	0.70123	0.21692	0.22379	1	0.0079772
Fleiss Kappa	0.6984293	0.22299	0.20763	1	0.0095418
Gwet AC1/AC2	0.7007792	0.2179	0.22119	1	0.0082164
BP Coefficient	0.7	0.2195	0.21688	1	0.0086216
Krippendorff Alpha	0.7099237	0.20501	0.2587	1	0.0053062

Figure 3.14: Agreement coefficients calculated with Program 3.7

Table 3.3: SAS/IML `agreecoeff3raw.sas` Library Functions and their Return Arguments

SAS/IML Function	Return Vectors	Content of Return Vectors				
		1	2	3	4	5
pa_coeff_raw	mout	pa	stderr_est	lcb	ucb	p_value
	nlabels	"Percent Agreement"	"Std Err"	"LCB"	"UCB"	"p-value"
bp_coeff_raw	mout	bp_coeff	stderr_est	lcb	ucb	p_value
	mlabels	"BP Coefficient"	"Std Err"	"LCB"	"UCB"	"p-value"
conger_kappa_raw	mout	conger_kappa_est	stderr_est	lcb	ucb	p_value
	mlabels	"Conger's Kappa"	"Std Err"	"LCB"	"UCB"	"p-value"
fleiss_kappa_raw	mout	fleiss_kappa	stderr_est	lcb	ucb	p_value
	mlabels	"Fleiss Kappa"	"Std Err"	"LCB"	"UCB"	"p-value"
gwet_ac1_raw	mout	gwet_ac1	stderr_est	lcb	ucb	p_value
	mlabels	"Gwet AC1/AC2"	"Std Err"	"LCB"	"UCB"	"p-value"
krippen_alpha_raw	mout	krippen_alpha	stderr_est	lcb	ucb	p_value
	mlabels	"Krippendorff Alpha"	"Std Err"	"LCB"	"UCB"	"p-value"

Table 3.4: SAS/IML `agreecoeff3dist.sas` Library Functions and their Return Arguments

SAS/IML Function	Return Vectors	Content of Return Vectors				
		1	2	3	4	5
pa_coeff_dist	mout	pa_coeff	stderr	lcb	ucb	p_value
	mlabels	"Percent Agreement"	"Std Err"	"LCB"	"UCB"	"p-value"
bp_coeff_dist	mout	bp_coeff	stderr	lcb	ucb	p_value
	mlabels	"BP Coefficient"	"Std Err"	"LCB"	"UCB"	"p-value"
fleiss_kappa_dist	mout	fleiss_kappa	stderr	lcb	ucb	p_value
	mlabels	"Fleiss Kappa"	"Std Err"	"LCB"	"UCB"	"p-value"
gwet_ac1_dist	mout	gwet_ac1	stderr	lcb	ucb	p_value
	mlabels	"Gwet AC1/AC2"	"Std Err"	"LCB"	"UCB"	"p-value"
krippen_alpha_dist	mout	krippen_alpha	stderr_est	lcb	ucb	p_value
	mlabels	"Krippendorff's Alpha"	"Std Err"	"LCB"	"UCB"	"p-value"

CHAPTER 4

Analysis of Quantitative Ratings

Contents

4.1   Introduction

Chapters 2 and 3 are devoted to inter-rater reliability assessment for categorical ratings. The methods discussed in these 2 chapters are different versions of chance-corrected agreement coefficients and do not apply to quantitative ratings. A fixed and predetermined set of categorical ratings is generally made available to all raters before the beginning of the inter-rater reliability experiment, whereas quantitative ratings are produced by individual raters during the rating process. Since the magnitude of quantitative ratings is known only after the experiment had taken place, the extent of agreement among raters is generally quantified with the Intraclass Correlation Coefficient (ICC). This chapter discusses how ICC can be computed with **SAS** .

An influential paper in the field of ICC as a measure of inter-rater reliability was produced by Shrout and Fleiss (1979) . These authors proposed 6 ICC statistics that are often used by researchers in various fields of research. **SAS** built-in procedures will not produce these 6 statistics as specified by the authors. However, a **SAS** macro named **INTRACC.SAS** and often used by researchers can be downloaded using the following link:

https://support.sas.com/kb/25/addl/fusion25031_1_intracc.sas.txt.

The use of this macro is reviewed in section 4.3. It is a well documented program and you can find more details about its use with the following link:

https://support.sas.com/kb/25/031.html.

Note that the **INTRACC.SAS** macro is solely based on the work of Shrout and Fleiss (1979), which has a few important limitations:

- The methods discussed by Shrout and Fleiss (1979) cannot deal with missing ratings, which are common in the field of inter-rater reliability.

- Shrout-Fleiss methods are limited to experiments where a single rating is associated with each subject. However, experiments where subjects are rated multiple times by the same rater are common in practice. The methods for computing ICC estimates must be sufficiently general to include these scenarios.

To deal with these problems, I developed 2 **SAS/IML** libraries of function modules named `icc1factor.sas` and `icc2x3.sas`, which can compute the ICC(1, 1), ICC(2, 1) and ICC(3, 1) statistics regardless of the number of measurements per subject and whether there are missing ratings or not. These libraries can be downloaded using the following links:

https://agreestat.com/books/sas2/chap4/icc1factor.sas,

https://agreestat.com/books/sas2/chap4/icc2x3.sas.

Section 4.4 provides a more detailed coverage of these 2 libraries and shows examples of their use.

4.2   **Intraclass Correlation: An Overview**

The analysis of quantitative measurements generally starts with a hypothetical statistical model that is assumed to describe your data reasonably well. Analysis of Variance (ANOVA) models are typically used to describe quantitative rating data. Shrout and Fleiss (1979) have defined the following 3 main ANOVA models[1]:

- *Model 1.* This is a one-factor ANOVA where the rating y_{ij} associated with subject i and rater j is assumed to be the sum of the expected score μ, the random i^{th} subject effect s_i and the random error effect e_{ij}. More formally, you have,

$$y_{ij} = \mu + s_i + e_{ij}, \qquad (4.2.1)$$

---

[1]These models are discussed in great details by Gwet (2021b)

where s_i follows the Normal distribution with mean 0 and variance σ_s^2, and e_{ij} follows the Normal distribution with mean 0 and variance σ_e^2. For this model, Shrout and Fleiss (1979) formulated an intraclass correlation coefficient referred to as $\text{ICC}(1,1)$.

- *Model 2.* This is two-way random effect ANOVA model, where the rating y_{ij} associated with subject i and rater j is assumed to be the sum of the expected score μ, the random i^{th} subject effect s_i, the random rater effect r_j, the subject-rater interaction $(sr)_{ij}$, and the random error effect e_{ij}. More formally, we have,

$$y_{ij} = \mu + s_i + r_j + (sr)_{ij} + e_{ij}, \qquad (4.2.2)$$

where s_i follows the Normal distribution with mean 0 and variance σ_s^2, the rater effect r_j follows the Normal distribution with mean 0 and variance σ_r^2, the interaction effect $(sr)_{ij}$ follows the Normal distribution with mean 0 and variance σ_{sr}^2. Finally the error effect follows the Normal distribution with mean 0 and variance σ_e^2. The subject and rater effects are pairwise independent. For this model, Shrout and Fleiss (1979) formulated an intraclass correlation coefficient referred to as $\text{ICC}(2,1)$.

- *Model 3.* This is two-way mixed effect ANOVA model, where the rating y_{ij} associated with subject i and rater j is assumed to be the sum of the expected score μ, the random i^{th} subject effect s_i, the fixed rater effect r_j, the subject-rater interaction $(sr)_{ij}$, and the random error effect e_{ij}. More formally, we have,

$$y_{ij} = \mu + s_i + r_j + (sr)_{ij} + e_{ij}, \qquad (4.2.3)$$

where s_i follows the Normal distribution with mean 0 and variance σ_s^2, the rater effects r_j $(j = 1, \cdots, r)$ sum to 0, the interaction effect $(sr)_{ij}$ follows the Normal distribution with mean 0 and variance σ_{sr}^2 and sum to 0 for any given subject i. Finally the error effect follows the Normal distribution with mean 0 and variance σ_e^2. For this model, Shrout and Fleiss (1979) formulated an intraclass correlation coefficient referred to as ICC(3, 1).

All 3 intraclass correlation coefficients ICC(1, 1), ICC(2, 1) and ICC(3, 1) are implemented in the **SAS** macro **INTRACC.SAS**. Shrout and Fleiss (1979) proposed 3 additional intraclass correlations named ICC(1, k), ICC(2, k) and ICC(3, k) and which aim at quantifying the intraclass correlation based on the analysis of the mean of k ratings, as opposed to the analysis individual ratings. These k-ICC estimates are implemented in the **INTRACC.SAS** macro as well.

> *I do not recommend using the k-ICC coefficients and will not discuss them in details in this book. Their use does not appear to be based on any sound theoretical or substantive ground.*

Some researchers even have a tendency of using k-ICC coefficients for the sole purpose of obtaining larger ICC estimates and claiming to have obtained good reliability. Shrout and Fleiss (1979) indicate that "*More typically, an investigator decides to use a mean as a unit of analysis because the individual rating is too unreliable.*" If the individual rating is too unreliable, then it is what it is and this should be reported. The average rating cannot be used as a surrogate for the individual rating and still lead to a valid measure of the extent of agreement among raters. Even if the study objective is to evaluate teams of physicians - an example used by Shrout and Fleiss (1979) - rather than individual physicians, the mean rating will still not be the answer. One should build a team consensus instead, either by reconciling differences through discussions or by using the first principal component[2]. An average of independent individual ratings within a team cannot be seen as a team attribute and will not lead to a valid inter-team reliability.

---

[2]For more details on the use of principal component analysis in inter-rater reliability assessment, see (Gwet, 2021b, sectin 9.4)

4.3   Using the INTRACC.SAS Macro

Let us consider the small dataset of Table 4.1. The **SAS** program 4.1 reads this data and computes all intraclass correlation coefficients described by Shrout and Fleiss (1979). The outcome of this program is shown in Figures 4.2 and 4.1.

Although the input dataset is supplied to the program in the same way it is presented in Table 4.1 (c.f. lines #10 through #15), the program must read it in such a way that the created **SAS** dataset will look like the table in Figure 4.2. This is the only format that the **INTRACC.SAS** macro can accept. The use of this format is likely a constraint imposed by the **GLM** procedure used in the macro. The main advantage of this format is to allow you to analyze several rating variables simultaneously. This feature can prove useful if the subjects are rated on 2 or 3 different characteristics.

Line #22 is where the program includes the **INTRACC.SAS** macro. Make sure you specify the directory into which you downloaded the macro. For this program, this directory is `c:\kgwet\sas2\chap4`. In line #23 the **INTRACC.SAS** macro is called with the minimum number of parameters. The rating dataset **sfdata**, the dependent variable **score** containing the ratings, the variable representing the target (or subject) named **subject**, and the rater variable called **judge**. The results produced by this program are shown in Figure 4.1. The 3 most important numbers on this output are the following:

- "Shrout-Fleiss reliability: single score," or $ICC(1,1) = 0.16574$.

- "Shrout-Fleiss reliability: random set," or $ICC(2,1) = 0.28976$.

- "Shrout-Fleiss reliability: fixed set," or $ICC(3,1) = 0.71484$.

Before deciding which of the 3 statistics to use, you need to refer to the assumptions that underly the associated ANOVA model. $ICC(3,1)$ for example will not be appropriate if you want your analysis to apply to raters beyond those who participated in the experiment. Similarly, ICC(2, 1) should be considered only if each rater rated all subjects. If the subjects were rated by different groups of raters, then you will want to consider ICC(1, 1).

If you are interested in the other statistics, you may read the paper of Shrout and Fleiss (1979) as well as the macro documentation.

Table 4.1: Ratings of 6 subjects generated by 4 raters[a]

	Judge			
Target	1	2	3	4
1	9	2	5	8
2	6	1	3	2
3	8	4	6	8
4	7	1	2	6
5	10	5	6	9
6	6	2	4	7

[a]Data from Shrout and Fleiss (1979, Page #423)

Program 4.1. Using the **INTRACC.SAS** macro and Table 4.1 data to compute intraclass correlation coefficients (*Download this program with the link:* https://agreestat.com/books/sas2/chap4/prg4shrout.sas)

```
01   data sfdata(drop=i);
02      do i=1 to 6;
03        input subject@@;
04        do judge=1 to 4;
05          input score@@;
06          output;
07        end;
08      end;
09   datalines;
10   1  9 2 5 8
11   2  6 1 3 2
12   3  8 4 6 8
13   4  7 1 2 6
```

```
14   5 10 5 6 9
15   6  6 2 4 7
16   ;
17
18   ods pdf file="c:\kgwet\sas2\chap4\shroutfleiss.pdf"
19        style=Ocean;
20     proc print data=sfdata;run;
21     /* Define the INTRACC macro */
22     %inc "c:\kgwet\sas2\chap4\intracc.sas";
23     %intracc(data=sfdata,depvar=score,target=subject,
24        rater=judge);
25   ods pdf close;
```

Intraclass Correlations for Inter-Rater Reliability
Calculate all reliabilities in one fell swoop

NAME	msw	msb	wms	ems	edf	bms	bdf	jms	jdf	k	theta
score	6.26389	11.2417	6.26389	1.01944	15	11.2417	5	32.4861	3	4	0.19867

NAME	Winer reliability: single score	Winer reliability: mean of k scores	Shrout-Fleiss reliability: single score	Shrout-Fleiss reliability: random set	Shrout-Fleiss reliability: fixed set
score	0.16574	0.44280	0.16574	0.28976	0.71484

NAME	Shrout-Fleiss reliability: mean k scores	Shrout-Fleiss rel: rand set mean k scrs	Shrout-Fleiss rel: fxd set mean k scrs
score	0.44280	0.62005	0.90932

Figure 4.1: Various intraclass correlation coefficients and related statistics produced by Program 4.1

Obs	subject	judge	score
1	1	1	9
2	1	2	2
3	1	3	5
4	1	4	8
5	2	1	6
6	2	2	1
7	2	3	3
8	2	4	2
9	3	1	8
10	3	2	4
11	3	3	6
12	3	4	8
13	4	1	7
14	4	2	1
15	4	3	2
16	4	4	6
17	5	1	10
18	5	2	5
19	5	3	6
20	5	4	9
21	6	1	6
22	6	2	2
23	6	3	4
24	6	4	7

Figure 4.2: Input dataset used in 4.1

4.4   The SAS/IML Function Modules for ICC

Consider the rating dataset of Table 4.2. The 5 subjects that participated in the experiment were rated 3 times by each of the 4 judges. The analysis of such a dataset was not addressed by Shrout and Fleiss (1979) and the `INTRACC.SAS` macro cannot adequately process it. In section 4.4.1, I will describe the `icc1factor.sas` macro needed to analyze one-way ANOVA models. Sections 4.4.2 and 4.4.3 discuss the `icc2x3.sas` macro needed for analyzing two-way Random and Mixed ANOVA models respectively.

Table 4.2: Ratings assigned to 6 subjects by 4 judges, with 3 ratings per subject and per judge

Target	Judge			
	J1	J2	J3	J4
1	6.0	1.0	3.0	2
1	6.5	3.0	3.0	4
1	4.0	3.0	5.5	4
5	10.0	5.0	6.0	9
5	9.0	4.5	5.0	9
5	9.5	4.0	6.6	8
4	6.0	2.0	4.0	7
4	7.0	1.0	3.0	6
4	8.0	2.5	4.0	5
2	9.0	2.0	5.0	8
2	7.0	1.0	2.0	6
2	8.0	2.0	2.0	7
3	10.0	5.0	6.0	9
3	7.0	4.0	6.0	5
3	8.0	4.0	6.0	8

4.4.1   One-Factor ANOVA Models

If Table 4.2 ratings must be described with a one-way ANOVA model, you will have 2 options. You can either consider a random subject effect model (or Model 1A) or a random rater effect model (or Model 1B). For Model 1A, a typical score y_{ijk} associated with subject i, rater j and measurement (or replicate) k is mathematically described as follows:

$$y_{ijk} = \mu + s_i + e_{ijk}, \qquad (4.4.1)$$

where s_i is the random subject effect that follows the Normal distribution with mean 0 and variance σ_s^2 and e_{ijk} is the random error term that follows the Normal distribution with mean 0 and variance σ_e^2. This model is indicated if the subjects are rated by different groups of judges.

For Model 1B, score y_{ijk} is mathematically described as follows:

$$y_{ijk} = \mu + r_j + e_{ijk}, \qquad (4.4.2)$$

where r_i is the random rater effect that follows the Normal distribution with mean 0 and variance σ_r^2 and e_{ijk} is the random error term that follows the Normal distribution with mean 0 and variance σ_e^2. This model is indicated if the judges did not rate the same subject sample. That is, the subjects rated by the judges differ by design and not because of random missing ratings.

Gwet (2021b) provides a more detailed discussion of these 2 models and describes the methods for estimating the variance components as well as the associated intraclass correlation coefficients.

The `icc1factor.sas` library contains several functions. However, the 2 main functions to know are `icc1a_fn()` for Model 1A analysis and `icc1b_fn()` for Model 1B analysis.

- `icc1a_fn()`

Input: The only input parameter is the mandatory input dataset of ratings organized as shown in Table 4.2.

Return: This function returns a list of 2 vectors named `outstats` and `outlabels`.

The elements of vector `outstats` are `sig2s` (subject variance component), `sig2e` (error variance component), `icc1a` (ICC based on Model 1A), `n` (number of subjects), `r` (number of raters), `max_rep` (maximum number of ratings per subject & per rater), `min_rep` (minimum number of ratings per subject & per rater), `Mtot` (total number of ratings from all raters), `ov_mean` (overall mean score).

Vector `outlabels` contains labels for the `outstats` vector elements.

- `icc1b_fn()`

Input: The only input parameter is the mandatory input dataset of ratings organized as shown in Table 4.2.

Return: This function returns a list of 2 vectors named `outstats` and `outlabels`.

Vector `outstats` elements are `sig2r` (rater variance component), `sig2e` (error variance component), `icc1b` (ICC based on Model 1B), `n` (number of subjects), `r` (number of raters), `max_rep` (maximum number of ratings per subject & per rater), `min_rep` (minimum number of ratings per subject & per rater), `Mtot` (total number of ratings from all raters), `ov_mean` (overall mean score).

Vector `outlabels` contains labels for the `outstats` vector elements.

Program 4.2 shows how the SAS/IML library `icc1factor.sas` can be used to analyze Table 4.2 ratings under both models 1A and 1B to obtain the 2 tables in Figures 4.3 and 4.4.

Line #26 is where you include the `icc1factor.sas` library of SAS/IML function modules. You need to replace my directory `c:\kgwet\chap4` with the directory where you keep the library file. Lines #33 through #45 deal with the Model 1A analysis, whereas Model 1B analysis is performed in the segment of the program that goes from lines #47 through #59. Using the `icc1factor.sas` library makes the implementation of the one-factor analysis straightforward. As an exercise, you may replicate the analysis Table 4.1 data using this library and compare your results with those of Figure 4.1.

It follows from Figure 4.3 that the subject and error variance components are respectively given by $\widehat{\sigma}_s^2 = 1.53$ and $\widehat{\sigma}_e^2 = 4.940$. The associated intraclass correlation coefficient is $ICC(1A, 1) = 0.237$ and the 95% confidence interval is $(0.044; 0.762)$. The last 2 columns of this table show the p-values for various levels of the hypothesized intraclass correlation[3]. A p-value smaller than 0.05 is an indication that the data is consistent with the hypothesis that the "true" ICC exceed the hypothesized value of `Rho`.

Figure 4.4 shows that under Model 1B, the rater and error variance components are respectively estimated at $\widehat{\sigma}_r^2 = 4.208$ and $\widehat{\sigma}_e^2 = 2.9759$. The intraclass correlation coefficient is $ICC(1B, 1) = 0.5857$ and the associated 95% is $(0, 1)$. This confidence interval has the maximum width of 1 due primarily to the small number of subjects and the small number of measurements per rater and per subject. Finally, the last 2 columns of the table show the p-values associated with the ICC for various levels of the hypothesized ICC. The hypothesized ICC of `Rho=0.3` led to a p-value of 0.039, which is smaller than 0.05. Therefore, the reported data is consistent with the hypothesis that the "true" ICC exceeds 0.3.

Note that the ICC under Model 1A represents a measure of inter-rater reliability, whereas under Model 1B it represents a measure of intra-rater reliability. When the subject is the only random factor considered in the model[4], then ICC

---

[3]This p-value quantifies the likelihood that the "true" ICC exceeds the hypothesized value shown in the next to last column.

[4]This will be the case if the subjects are rated by different raters.

is the correlation coefficient between 2 raters. If the rater is the only random factor considered[5], then ICC will be the correlation coefficient between 2 measurements given a subject and a rater. This issue is discussed mathematically in Gwet (2021b).

Program 4.2. Calculating Intraclass Correlation Coefficients (ICC) under the one-factor ANOVA model. (*You may download this program using the following link:* https://agreestat.com/books/sas2/chap4/prg4icc1.sas)

```
01   options mprint;
02   proc datasets library=WORK kill; run; quit;
03   data ratings;
04       input target J1 J2 J3 J4;
05       datalines;
06        1  6.0 1.0 3.0  2
07        1  6.5 3.0 3.0  4
08        1  4.0 3.0 5.5  4
09        5 10.0 5.0 6.0  9
10        5  9.0 4.5 5.0  9
11        5  9.5 4.0 6.6  8
12        4  6.0 2.0 4.0  7
13        4  7.0 1.0 3.0  6
14        4  8.0 2.5 4.0  5
15        2  9.0 2.0 5.0  8
16        2  7.0 1.0 2.0  6
17        2  8.0 2.0 2.0  7
18        3 10.0 5.0 6.0  9
19        3  7.0 4.0 6.0  5
20        3  8.0 4.0 6.0  8
21   ;
22
23   ods pdf file="c:\kgwet\chap4\icc1.pdf" style=Ocean;
24
25   proc iml;
26       %inc "c:\kgwet\chap4\icc1factor.sas";
27       use ratings;
28           read all var _NUM_ into mratings[colname=rNames];
29       close ratings;
```

---

[5]This will often be the case if the same group of raters rate different subjects by design.

```
30        title "Input ratings";
31        print mratings;
32
33        /*- Model 1A --*/
34
35        title "ICC under 1-Factor Model 1A";
36        icc1alst = icc1a_fn(mratings);
37        ci1alst = ci_ICC1a(mratings);
38        pval1a = pval_ICC1a(mratings);
39        icc1aStats = icc1alst$1;icc1aLabels= icc1alst$2;
40            mattrib icc1aStats r=icc1aLabels;
41        ci1a = "("+strip(char(round(ci1alst$1,1/10**4)))+" to "+
42            strip(char(round(ci1alst$2,1/10**4)))+")";
43        mattrib pval1a c={"Rho","Pval"};
44        print icc1aStats[l="Stats (Model 1A)"]
45                ci1a[l="ICC Confidence Interval"] pval1a[l=""];
46
47        /*- Model 1B --*/
48
49        title "ICC under 1-Factor Model 1B";
50        icc1blst = icc1b_fn(mratings);
51        ci1blst = ci_ICC1b(mratings);
52        pval1b = pval_ICC1b(mratings);
53        icc1bStats = icc1blst$1;icc1bLabels= icc1blst$2;
54            mattrib icc1bStats r=icc1bLabels;
55        ci1b = "("+strip(char(ci1blst$1))+" to " +
56                strip(char(ci1blst$2))+")";
57        mattrib pval1b c={"Rho","Pval"};
58        print icc1bStats[l="Stats (Model 1B)"]
59            ci1b[l="ICC Confidence Interval"] pval1b[l=""];
60  quit;
61  ods pdf close;
```

Stats (Model 1A)		ICC Confidence Interval	Rho	Pval
SubVar: sig2s	1.5308838	(0.0444 to 0.7624)	0	0.0024022
ErrorVar: sig2e	4.9395606		0.1	0.1039507
ICC	0.2365964		0.3	0.5505311
#subjects: n	5		0.5	0.8338861
#raters: r	4		0.7	0.9563186
Max #Obs/subj	3		0.9	0.996347
Min #Obs/subj	3			
Total #Obs	60			
Mean Rating	5.385			

Figure 4.3: Intraclass Correlation Coefficients (ICC) under model 1A, calculated with Program 4.2

Stats (Model 1B)		ICC Confidence Interval	Rho	Pval
RaterVar: sig2r	4.207545	(0 to 1)	0	1.3322E-9
ErrorVar: sig2e	2.975881		0.1	0.0001139
ICC	0.5857296		0.3	0.0385711
#subjects: n	5		0.5	0.255916
#raters: r	4		0.7	0.6069478
Max #Obs/subj	3		0.9	0.9206286
Min #Obs/subj	3			
Total #Obs	60			
Mean Rating	5.385			

Figure 4.4: Intraclass Correlation Coefficients (ICC) under model 1B, calculated with Program 4.2

4.4.2   *Two-Factor Random ANOVA Models*

In section 4.4.1, I reviewed 2 one-factor ANOVA models for estimating the ICC. Model 1A is a one-way random subject effect model, whereas Model 1B is a one-way random rater effect model. Model 1A is needed for quantifying inter-rater reliability and Model 1B for quantifying intra-rater reliability. However, a dataset such as that of Table 4.2 containing several subjects and several measurements per subject can be used to compute both the inter-rater and the intra-rater reliability coefficients. To achieve this goal, you need to hypothesize a two-way model that involves both the rater and the subject effects. It is also common to add the subject-rater interaction effect, since different raters may look at the same subjects differently.

In a two-way ANOVA model, the subject and rater effects can both be random, in which case you will have a two-way random effect model. This model is discussed in this section. Alternatively, the subject effect will be random and the rater will be fixed, in which case you will have a mixed effect model. Mixed-effect models are discussed in section 4.4.3.

In a two-way random effect model, a typical score y_{ijk} associated with subject i, rater j and measurement k is described mathematically as follows:

$$y_{ijk} = \mu + s_i + r_j + (sr)_{ij} + e_{ijk}, \tag{4.4.3}$$

where μ is the expected score, s_i the random subject effect, r_j the random rater effect, $(sr)_{ij}$ the random subject-rater interaction effect and e_{ijk} the error effect. The subject, rater, interaction and error effects are all assumed to follow a Normal distribution with mean 0 and variances of σ_s^2, σ_r^2, σ_{sr}^2 and σ_e^2 respectively. There are a few other assumptions that apply to these random effects. A more detailed discussion can be found in Gwet (2021b). .

Note that model 4.4.3 reduces to model 2 (case #2) of Shrout and Fleiss (1979) is there is a single measurement per subject. However, with multiple measurements per subject model 4.4.3 allows for the calculation of both inter-rater and intra-rater reliability coefficients. The mathematical formulation of these ICC parameters and associated computation methods are extensively discussed in Gwet (2021b). In this section, I will focus on the use of the `icc2x3.sas` library to perform the required analysis. Under Model 2, I will denote the inter-rater reliability ICC by $ICC_r(2,1)$, whereas the intra-rater reliability ICC is denoted by $ICC_a(2,1)$.

For the sake of analyzing Table 4.2 data for example under model 4.4.3, 5 key functions from the `icc2x3.sas` library are useful:

- `icc2_inter_fn()`

  This function computes both the inter-rater and intra-rater reliability coefficients and takes an input dataset organized as shown in Table 4.2. It is called as follows:

  `icc2lst = icc2_inter_fn(inputfile);`

  where `icc2lst` is a list of 2 vectors. The first vector contains 12 statistics and the second the associated labels. The 12 statistics of the first vector are the following:

`sig2s`: Subject variance component	`n`: Number of subjects	
`sig2r`: Rater variance component	`r`: Number of raters	
`sig2e`: Error variance component	`max`: Max ratings/subject	
`sig2sr`: Interaction var. component	`min`: Min ratings/subject	
`icc2r`: Inter-rater ICC	`Mtot`: Total # of ratings	
`icc2a`: Intra-rater ICC	`yMean`: Overall mean rating	

- `ci_ICC2r_inter(dfrac,conflev=0.95)`: This function computes both the lower and upper bounds of the inter-rater ICC. It takes one mandatory parameter `dfra`, the input dataset, and one optional parameter `conflev` representing the confidence level with a default value 0.95. You would call it as follows:

  `ci2rlst = ci_ICC2r_inter(inputfile);`

  `ci2rlst` is a list containing the lower bound and the upper bound.

- `pval_ICC2r_inter()` This functions returns a matrix whose first column contains the hypothesized ICC values of 0, 0.1, 0.3, 0.5, 0.7 and 0.9, and whose second column contains the associated p-values for the inter-rater ICC. It is called as follows: `pval2r = pval_ICC2r_inter(mratings)`.

- `ci_ICC2a_inter(dfra,conflev=0.95)`: This function computes both the lower and upper bounds of the intra-rater ICC. It takes one mandatory parameter `dfra`, the input dataset, and one optional parameter `conflev` representing the confidence level with a default value 0.95. You would call it as follows:

  `ci2alst = ci_ICC2a_inter(mratings);`

  `ci2rlst` is a list containing the lower bound and the upper bound.

- `pvals_ICC2a_inter(dfra,rho_zeros=0)`: This function performs p-value calculations for the intra-rater Intraclass Correlation Coefficient $ICC_a(2,1)$ associated with model 4.4.3 with interaction. The input dataset `dfra` is a mandatory parameter, whereas `rho_zeros` is an optional parameter containing a vector of hypothesized ICC values with a default value of 0. It can be called as follows:

  `pval2a = pvals_ICC2a_inter(mratings,t(do(0,0.9,0.1)));`

Program 4.3 shows how the key functions in the library `icc2x3.sas` can be used to analyze Table 4.2 data based on model 4.4.3. The results produced by this program are presented in Figures 4.5 and 4.6.

It follows from Figure 4.5 that the inter-rater and intra-rater reliability coefficients are respectively given by $ICC_r(2,1) = 0.233$ and $ICC_a(2,1) = 0.846$. In addition to the 95% confidence intervals, you also find estimates of the variance components and other statistics on the output. Figure 4.6 on the other hand shows p-values for both the inter-rater and intra-rater ICCs.

- The inter-rater reliability ICC is low. Figure 4.6 indicates that even for a low hypothesized inter-rater ICC of 0.1, the p-value is $0.14 > 0.05$. That is, the data does not support the hypothesis that the "true" inter-rater ICC exceeds 0.1.

- The intra-rater reliability ICC is high. Again, Figure 4.6 indicates that even if the hypothesized intra-rater ICC is as high as 0.6, the p-value of 0.012 remains below 5%. Therefore, the data supports the hypothesis that the "true" ICC exceeds 0.6.

Program 4.3. Calculating Intraclass Correlation Coefficients (ICC) under the two-way ANOVA model with random effects. (*You may download this program using the following link:* https://agreestat.com/books/sas2/chap4/prg4icc2.sas)

```
01   proc datasets library=WORK kill; run; quit;
02   data ratings;
03     input target J1 J2 J3 J4;
04     datalines;
05   1  6.0 1.0 3.0  2
06   1  6.5 3.0 3.0  4
07   1  4.0 3.0 5.5  4
08   5 10.0 5.0 6.0  9
09   5  9.0 4.5 5.0  9
10   5  9.5 4.0 6.6  8
11   4  6.0 2.0 4.0  7
12   4  7.0 1.0 3.0  6
13   4  8.0 2.5 4.0  5
14   2  9.0 2.0 5.0  8
15   2  7.0 1.0 2.0  6
16   2  8.0 2.0 2.0  7
17   3 10.0 5.0 6.0  9
18   3  7.0 4.0 6.0  5
19   3  8.0 4.0 6.0  8
20   ;
21
22   ods pdf file="c:\kgwet\chap4\icc2.pdf" style=Ocean;
23
24   proc iml;
25     %inc "C:\kgwet\chap4\icc2x3.sas";
26     use ratings;
27       read all var _NUM_ into mratings[colname=rNames];
```

```
28    close ratings;
29    title "Input ratings";
30    print mratings[L=""];
31    /*- Model 2 --*/
32    title "ICC under 2-Factor Random Model 2";
33    icc2lst = icc2_inter_fn(mratings);
34    ci2rlst = ci_ICC2r_inter(mratings);
35    pval2r = pval_ICC2r_inter(mratings);
36
37    ci2alst=ci_ICC2a_inter(mratings);
38    pval2a=pvals_ICC2a_inter(mratings,t(do(0,0.9,0.1)));
39
40    icc2Stats = icc2lst$1;icc2rLabels= icc2lst$2;
41    mattrib icc2Stats r=icc2rLabels;
42    ci2r = "("+strip(char(round(ci2rlst$1,1/10**4)))+" to "+
43              strip(char(round(ci2rlst$2,1/10**4)))+")";
44    ci2a = "("+strip(char(round(ci2alst$1,1/10**4)))+" to "+
45              strip(char(round(ci2alst$2,1/10**4)))+")";
46    ci = ci2r//ci2a;
47
48    mattrib pval2r c={"Rho","Pval(Inter-rater)"};
49    mattrib pval2a c={"Rho","Pval(Intra-rater"};
50
51    varComp = icc2Stats[1:4];vcLabels=icc2rLabels[1:4];
52    dStats = icc2Stats[7:12];dLabels=icc2rLabels[7:12];
53    iccstats=icc2Stats[5:6]; iccLabels=icc2rLabels[5:6];
54    mattrib dStats r=dLabels;
55    mattrib varComp r=vcLabels;
56    mattrib iccstats r=iccLabels c="ICC";
57    print dStats[L="Descriptive Stats"]
58    varComp[l="Variance Components"];
59    print iccstats[l="Intraclass Correlations"]
60          ci[l="Confidence Intervals"];
61    print pval2r[L=""] pval2a[L=""];
62 quit;
63 ods pdf close;
```

Descriptive Stats		Variance Components	
#Subjects:n	5	SubVar:sig2s	1.755463
#Raters:r	4	RaterVar:sig2r	4.2562963
#MaxObs/Subj	3	ErrorVar:sig2e	1.1618333
#MinObs/Subj	3	InterVar:sig2sr	0.3609259
#TotObs	60		
Mean Ratings	5.385		

Intraclass Correlations	ICC	Confidence Intervals
ICC(Inter):icc2r	0.2329894	(0.0212 to 0.7536)
ICC(Intra):icc2a	0.8457986	(0.6412 to 0.9665)

Figure 4.5: Intraclass Correlation Coefficients (ICC) under model 2, calculated with Program 4.3

Rho	Pval(Inter-rater)	Rho	Pval(Intra-rater
0	0.0007169	0	8.48E-10
0.1	0.1420562	0.1	3.8945E-8
0.3	0.608955	0.2	1.0028E-6
0.5	0.8502411	0.3	0.0000168
0.7	0.958985	0.4	0.0001986
0.9	0.9964485	0.5	0.0017672
		0.6	0.0121553
		0.7	0.0649494
		0.8	0.2612945
		0.9	0.7104248

Figure 4.6: P-values associated with the ICCs under model 2, calculated with Program 4.3

4.4.3   *Two-Factor Mixed ANOVA Models*

In a two-way mixed effect model, a typical score y_{ijk} associated with subject i, rater j and measurement k is described mathematically as follows:

$$y_{ijk} = \mu + s_i + r_j + (sr)_{ij} + e_{ijk}, \tag{4.4.4}$$

where μ is the expected score, s_i the random subject effect, r_j the fixed rater effect, $(sr)_{ij}$ the random subject-rater interaction effect and e_{ijk} the error effect. The subject, interaction and error effects are all assumed to follow the Normal distribution with the same mean 0 and variances of σ_s^2, σ_{sr}^2 and σ_e^2 respectively. Assuming that r raters and n subjects participated in the experiment, then all r rater effects and nr interaction effects are assumed to meet the following conditions:

$$\sum_{j=1}^{r} r_j = 0 \ \ and \ \sum_{j=1}^{r} (sr)_{ij} = 0, \ for \ any \ subject \ i. \tag{4.4.5}$$

There are a few other independence assumptions related to the different random effects that apply. A more detailed discussion can be found in Gwet (2021b).

Models 4.4.3 and 4.4.4 are very similar. The only exceptions are the rater effects, which are fixed in the mixed effects model and the conditions of equation 4.4.5 that must be satisfied. Again, model 4.4.4 generalizes model 2 (case #3) of Shrout and Fleiss (1979) , which is a special case based on a single measurement per subject. The generalized model 4.4.4 allows for the calculation of both inter-rater and intra-rater reliability coefficients with the same dataset.

To analyze Table 4.2 data under model 4.4.4, 5 key functions from the `icc2x3.sas` library are useful:

- `icc3_inter_fn(dfra)`

This function computes both the inter-rater and intra-rater reliability coefficients under Model 4.4.4 and takes an input dataset `dfra` organized as in Table 4.2. You would call this function as follows:

$$\text{icc3lst = icc3\_inter\_fn(mratings);}$$

where `icc3lst` is a list of 2 vectors. The first vector contains 12 statistics and the second the associated labels. The 12 statistics of the first vector are the following:

`sig2s`: Subject variance component	`n`: Number of subjects
`sig2e`: Error variance component	`r`: Number of raters
`sig2sr`: Interaction var. component	`max`: Max ratings/subject
`icc3r`: Inter-rater ICC	`min`: Min ratings/subject
`icc3a`: Intra-rater ICC	`Mtot`: Total # of ratings
	`yMean`: Overall mean rating

- `ci_ICC3r_inter(dfra,conflev=0.95)`: This function computes both the lower and upper confidence bounds of the inter-rater ICC. It takes one mandatory parameter `dfra`, which is the input dataset and one optional parameter `conflev` representing the confidence level with a default value of 0.95. To obtain the confidence interval, you would need to call this function as follows: `ci3rlst = ci_ICC3r_inter(inputfile);` where `ci3rlst` is a list containing the lower and the upper confidence bounds.

- `pvals_ICC3r_inter(dfra,rho_zeros=0)`: This function performs p-value calculations for the inter-rater ICC denoted by $ICC_r(3,1)$ and associated with model 4.4.4 with interaction. The input dataset `dfra` is a mandatory parameter, whereas `rho_zeros` is an optional parameter containing a vector of hypothesized ICC values for which a p-value is computed. It has a default value of 0. This function can be called as follows:

$$\text{pval3r = pvals\_ICC3r\_inter(mratings,t(do(0,0.9,0.1)));}$$

where `pval3r` is a two-column matrix with hypothesized values in the first column and the associated p-values in the second.

- `ci_ICC3a_inter(dfra,conflev=0.95)`: This function computes both the lower and upper confidence bounds of the intra-rater ICC denoted by $ICC_a(3,1)$ and associated with model 4.4.4 with interaction. It takes one mandatory parameter `dfra`, which is the input dataset, and one optional parameter `conflev` representing the confidence level with a default value of 0.95. You would call this function with the following commands:

  ```
  ci3alst = ci_ICC2a_inter(mratings);
  ```

  where `ci2rlst` is a list containing the lower and the upper confidence bounds.

- `pvals_ICC3a_inter(dfra,gam_zeros=0)`: This function performs p-value calculations for the intra-rater Intraclass Correlation Coefficient $ICC_a(3,1)$ associated with model 4.4.4 with interaction. The input dataset `dfra` is a mandatory parameter, whereas `rho_zeros` is an optional parameter containing a vector of hypothesized ICC values with a default value of 0. This function can be called as follows:

  ```
  pval3a = pvals_ICC3a_inter(mratings,t(do(0,0.9,0.1)));
  ```

Program 4.4 shows you how the library `icc2x3.sas` is used for analyzing Table 4.2 rating data based on the mixed effects model 4.4.4. The results produced by this program are shown in Figures 4.7 and 4.8. Figure 4.7 reveals that the inter-rater ICC based on model 4.4.4 is $ICC_r(3,1) = 0.522$ and the intra-rater ICC equals $ICC_a(3,1) = 0.654$. The different variance components used in the calculation are displayed in the same table. It follows from Figure 4.8 that the inter-rater p-value remains below 0.05 for hypothesized "true" ICC vlaues smaller than 0.2. That is, you can claim with high confidence that the "true" inter-rater ICC exceeds 0.2. Similarly, for hypothesized ICC values smaller than 0.3, the intra-rater ICC is smaller than 0.05 and with high confidence you may claim that the "true" intra-rater ICC exceeds 0.3.

Program 4.4. Calculating Intraclass Correlation Coefficients (ICC) under the two-way ANOVA model with mixed effects. (*You may download this program using the following link:* https://agreestat.com/books/sas2/chap4/prg4icc3.sas)

```
01  proc datasets library=WORK kill; run; quit;
02  data ratings;
03    input target J1 J2 J3 J4;
04    datalines;
05    1  6.0 1.0 3.0  2
06    1  6.5 3.0 3.0  4
07    1  4.0 3.0 5.5  4
08    5 10.0 5.0 6.0  9
09    5  9.0 4.5 5.0  9
10    5  9.5 4.0 6.6  8
11    4  6.0 2.0 4.0  7
12    4  7.0 1.0 3.0  6
13    4  8.0 2.5 4.0  5
14    2  9.0 2.0 5.0  8
15    2  7.0 1.0 2.0  6
16    2  8.0 2.0 2.0  7
17    3 10.0 5.0 6.0  9
18    3  7.0 4.0 6.0  5
19    3  8.0 4.0 6.0  8
20  ;
21
22  ods pdf file="c:\kgwet\chap4\icc3.pdf" style=Ocean;
23
24  proc iml;
25    %inc "c:\kgwet\chap4\icc2x3.sas";
26    use ratings;
27      read all var _NUM_ into mratings[colname=rNames];
28    close ratings;
29    title "Input ratings";
30    print mratings[L=""];
31    /*- Model 3 --*/
32    title "ICC under 2-Factor Mixed Model 3";
33    icc3lst = icc3_inter_fn(mratings);
34    ci3rlst = ci_ICC3r_inter(mratings);
35    pval3r = pvals_ICC3r_inter(mratings,t(do(0,0.9,0.1)));
36
37    ci3alst=ci_ICC3a_inter(mratings);
```

```
38    pval3a=pvals_ICC3a_inter(mratings,t(do(0,0.9,0.1)));
39
40    icc3Stats = icc3lst$1;icc3rLabels= icc3lst$2;
41    mattrib icc3Stats r=icc3rLabels;
42    ci3r = "("+strip(char(round(ci3rlst$1,1/10**4)))+" to "+
43        strip(char(round(ci3rlst$2,1/10**4)))+")";
44    ci3a = "("+strip(char(round(ci3alst$1,1/10**4)))+" to "+
45        strip(char(round(ci3alst$2,1/10**4)))+")";
46    ci = ci3r//ci3a;
47
48    mattrib pval3r c={"Rho","Pval(Inter-rater)"};
49    mattrib pval3a c={"Rho","Pval(Intra-rater"};
50
51    varComp = icc3Stats[1:3];vcLabels=icc3rLabels[1:3];
52    iccstats =icc3Stats[4:5];iccLabels=icc3rLabels[4:5];
53    dStats = icc3Stats[6:11];dLabels=icc3rLabels[6:11];
54    mattrib dStats r=dLabels;
55    mattrib varComp r=vcLabels;
56    mattrib iccstats r=iccLabels c="ICC";
57    print dStats[L="Descriptive Stats"]
58    varComp[l="Variance Components"];
59    print iccstats[l="Intraclass Correlations"]
60    ci[l="Confidence Intervals"];
61    print pval3r[L=""] pval3a[L=""];
62 quit;
63 ods pdf close;
```

Descriptive Stats		Variance Components	
#Subjects:n	5	SubVar:sig2s	1.8665171
#Raters:r	4	ErrorVar:sig2e	1.1618333
#MaxObs/Subj	3	InterVar:sig2sr	0.3331624
#MinObs/Subj	3		
#TotObs	60		
Mean Ratings	5.385		

Intraclass Correlations	ICC	Confidence Intervals
ICC(Inter):icc3r	0.5222241	(0.2159 to 0.9141)
ICC(Intra):icc3a	0.6543719	(0.3179 to 0.9053)

Figure 4.7: Intraclass Correlation Coefficients (ICC) under model 4.4.4, calculated with Program 4.4

Rho	Pval(Inter-rater)	Rho	Pval(Intra-rater
0	0.0007169	0	0.0001608
0.1	0.003899	0.1	0.0010836
0.2	0.0231211	0.2	0.0053215
0.3	0.0812716	0.3	0.0201801
0.4	0.195163	0.4	0.0614152
0.5	0.3566127	0.5	0.1537315
0.6	0.5422549	0.6	0.3207314
0.7	0.7220157	0.7	0.5593996
0.8	0.8697836	0.8	0.8107675
0.9	0.9663463	0.9	0.9706063

Figure 4.8: P-values associated with the ICCs under model 4.4.4, calculated with Program 4.4

4.5 Finn Coefficient

Finn's agreement coefficient is a special inter-rater reliability coefficient proposed by Finn (1970), as an alternative to the more traditional intraclass correlation coefficient (ICC). The ICC approach to inter-rater reliability can fail. Failure will typically happened when the subject effect on ratings is small. A small subject effect violates a fundamental and often overlooked assumption of the ICC approach to inter-rater reliability, which requires the subject population to be diverse.

In section 4.5.1, I provide a more detailed discussion of the ICC problem that justifies the importance of Finn's coefficient. In section 4.5.2, I will describe the Finn's coefficient and show how to compute it with **SAS** .

4.5.1 *The Problem*

To see how the traditional ICC can fail, consider the rating data shown in Table 4.3. It is from an inter-rater reliability where 4 judges rated each of 5 subjects on 3 occasions. If the subjects were rated by different groups of 4 raters then inter-rater reliability may be quantified using a one-factor random subject ANOVA model (see equation 4.2.1). In this case, the error and subject variance components are respectively given by $\widehat{\sigma}_e^2 = 0.27659$ and $\widehat{\sigma}_s^2 = 0.00520$, which leads to ICC $= 0.01846$. If the same group of 4 raters rated all subjects, and are assumed to have been randomly selected from a larger population of raters, then inter-rater reliability may be quantified using a two-way random model (with or without interaction) of equation 4.2.2. In this case and assuming no interaction, the error, subject and rater variance components are respectively given by $\widehat{\sigma}_e^2 = 0.25679$, $\widehat{\sigma}_s^2 = 0.00685$, and $\widehat{\sigma}_r^2 = 0.02420$, which leads to ICC $= 0.02380$. Likewise, the assumption of mixed model of equation 4.2.3 yields ICC $= 0.02598$. Therefore, whichever method you use to compute the ICC will lead to a low inter-rater reliability coefficient.

The very low magnitude of all these ICC estimates is highly suspicious, and certainly not consistent with the perception you get after a visual exploration of the dataset. Table 4.3 suggests that the 4 raters agree to a large extent in the way they score the 5 subjects being examined. To see what is going on, consider the estimates based on model 4.2.1 for example. With an estimated value of 0.00520, the subject variance is too small compared to the variance component associated with the combined effect of raters and experimental errors, which is estimated at 0.27659. The ICC as a measure of reliability is based on the following logic:

> *If total variation is largely dominated by its subject's component, then the variation due to raters will be small and the raters will be deemed in agreement.*

However, this logic does not tell you what happens if the subjects do not generate much variation because they form a very homogeneous group. That is where the ICC approach might fail you.

All ANOVA models discussed in this chapter assume the subject effect to be random. Therefore, the group of subjects used in the inter-rater reliability experiment is assumed to be a representative sample of a larger population of subjects. The ratings assigned to these subjects are expected to vary from subject to subject and from rater to rater. Moreover, total variation is explained by several factors. These are the type of subjects being rated (it is the subject effect), the extent to which the raters agree (it is the rater effect), and by the measurement errors or experimental errors or reading errors (it is the error effect). The error effect can be minimized when the experiment is well designed. In this case, the two main contributing factors to rating variation remain the subject and the rater. You can see at this stage that a very homogeneous subject population makes it nearly impossible to obtain a high ICC.

Table 4.3: Ratings of 5 Subjects by 4 Judges

Subject	J1	J2	J3	J4	Row Variance
1	6	5.6	5	5	
1	5	5	5	5	0.2118
1	5	5	5	4	
5	6	6	5	5	
5	5	5	5	5	0.1875
5	5	5	5	4.5	
4	6	6	5	5	
4	5	5	5	5	0.1515
4	5	5	5	5	
2	6	6	5	5	
2	5	5	5	5	0.1515
2	5	5	5	5	
3	6	6	5	5	
3	5	5	5	5	0.6806
3	3.5	3.8	3.6	4.3	
Average					0.2766

4.5.2 The Solution

Table 4.4 used by Finn (1970) to illustrate his method, shows ratings that
5 judges assigned to 4 items. Each judge was expected to assign one of the
integer values (1, 2, 3, 4, 5) to each of the 4 items. Finn's method can be
summarized as follows:

- Compute all 4 row (or subject-level) variances[6]. For Table 4.4, the 4
  subject variances are 0.2, 0.0, 0.20, and 0.20.

- Average all 4 subject-level variances to obtain the mean subject variance

---

[6]Note that these are sample variances, which use 3 (i.e. $4 - 1$) in their denominators.

(MSV) of 0.15. This number tells you how far on average the rating from any given judge will stray away from the average rating. The smaller the mean subject variance, the higher the rater agreement.

- Compute the expected value that this mean subject variance would take if the ratings were assigned to subjects in a purely random manner. If q is the total number rating values the judges can use (in our case $q = 5$) then the mean subject variance under the assumption of random rating is $(q-1)(q+1)/12$. For Table 4.4, this expected mean subject variance is $(5-1)(5+1)/12 = (4 \times 6)/12 = 2$.

- Compute Finn's coefficient as follows:

$$\boxed{r_{\mathrm{F}} = 1 - \frac{Observed\ \mathrm{MSV}}{Expected\ \mathrm{MSV}}.} \qquad (4.5.1)$$

To compute this coefficient, several variances are first calculated at the subject level. Even when several measurements are taken on each subject as in Table 4.3, variances must still first be computed within the group of measurements associated with one subject. Hence, the name "Within-group inter-rater reliability" often used to designate Finn's coefficient.

Using equation 4.5.1 and Table 4.4 data, Finn's coefficient is calculated as $r_{\mathrm{F}} = 1 - 0.15/2 = 0.925$.

Program 4.4 shows you how to compute Finn's coefficient using Table 4.3 data and using **SAS/IML**. This program produces the results shown in Figure 4.9. This figure shows the input dataset, the observed Mean Subject Variance (MSV) also denoted by S^2, the expected MSV often denoted by S_{E}^2, the Finn's coefficient and the associated p-value. This p-value is calculated based on a resampling approach discussed by Gwet (2021b, chap. 7).

Table 4.4: Ratings of 4 Items by 5 Judges with a Positive Finn's Coefficient

	Judges					
Items	I	II	III	IV	V	Row Variance
A	2	2	3	2	2	0.20
B	2	2	2	2	2	0.00
C	2	2	2	2	1	0.20
D	1	2	2	2	2	0.20
Average						0.15

Program 4.5. SAS program for calculating Finn's agreement coefficient and the associated p-value. (*You may download this program using the following link:* https://agreestat.com/books/sas2/chap4/prg4finn.sas)

```
01   proc datasets library=WORK kill; run; quit;
02   data ratings;
03     input target J1 J2 J3 J4;
04     datalines;
05   1 6 5.6 5 5
06   1 5 5 5 5
07   1 5 5 5 4
08   5 6 6 5 5
09   5 5 5 5 5
10   5 5 5 5 4.5
11   4 6 6 5 5
12   4 5 5 5 5
13   4 5 5 5 5
14   2 6 6 5 5
15   2 5 5 5 5
16   2 5 5 5 5
17   3 6 6 5 5
18   3 5 5 5 5
19   3 3.5 3.8 3.6 4.3
20   ;
21
22   ods pdf file="c:\kgwet\chap4\finncoeff.pdf" style=Ocean;
```

```
23   proc iml;
24     use ratings;
25       read all var _NUM_ into mratings[colname=rNames];
26     close ratings;
27
28     start finn(xratings);
29     scores = t(unique(xratings[,2:ncol(xratings)]));
30     qscores = nrow(scores);
31     se2 = (qscores-1)*var(scores)/qscores;
32
33     tarvec = t(unique(xratings[,1]));
34     ntarget = nrow(tarvec);*number of targets/subjects;
35     rjudges = ncol(xratings)-1;*number of judges/raters;
36     s2i_vec = repeat(0,ntarget);
37     do itar=1 to ntarget;
38       idx = loc(xratings[,1]=tarvec[itar]);
39       tar_mat = xratings[idx,][,2:rjudges+1];
40       s2i_vec[itar] = var(colvec(tar_mat));
41     end;
42     s2 = s2i_vec[:];
43     fcoeff = 1-s2/se2;
44     return(fcoeff||s2||se2);
45   finish;
46
47   fstats = finn(mratings);
48   finn_coeff = fstats[1];s2=fstats[2];se2=fstats[3];
49
50   /* Computing the p-value of Finn's coefficient */
51
52   nboot = 2000;
53   nrounds = nrow(mratings);
54   scores = t(unique(mratings[,2:ncol(mratings)]));
55   tarvec = t(unique(mratings[,1]));/*vector of subject ids */
56   ntarget = nrow(mratings);*number of targets/subjects;
57   rjudges = ncol(mratings)-1;*number of judges/raters;
58   pval = 0;
59   do i=1 to nboot;
60     bsample = mratings[,1]||sample(scores,rjudges||nrounds);
61     finnstats = finn(bsample);
62     if finnstats[1]>fcoeff then pval=pval+1;
63   end;
64
65   print mratings s2 se2 finn_coeff pval;
```

```
66    quit;
67    ods pdf close;
```

mratings target	J1	J2	J3	J4	s2	se2	finn_coeff	pval
1	6	5.6	5	5	0.2765909	0.6995062	0.6045912	0
1	5	5	5	5				
1	5	5	5	4				
5	6	6	5	5				
5	5	5	5	5				
5	5	5	5	4.5				
4	6	6	5	5				
4	5	5	5	5				
4	5	5	5	5				
2	6	6	5	5				
2	5	5	5	5				
2	5	5	5	5				
3	6	6	5	5				
3	5	5	5	5				
3	3.5	3.8	3.6	4.3				

Figure 4.9: Finn's agreement coefficient calculated with Program 4.5

CHAPTER $\boxed{5}$

Analysis Techniques for Categorical Ratings

Contents

5.1 Introduction

This chapter addresses 2 specific and important issues related to the analysis of categorical ratings. The first issue is that of testing the difference of 2 chance-corrected agreement coefficients for statistical significance. The second issue is the benchmarking of chance-corrected agreement coefficients on existing benchmark scales proposed in the literature. Benchmarking consists of evaluating the magnitude of an agreement coefficient against standard levels so that researchers can label them as "low", "moderate" or "high." The statistical test of significance is discussed in section 5.2, whereas the benchmarking procedure is described in section 5.3.

5.2 Testing Differences for Statistical Significance

The problem addressed in this section is that of comparing 2 agreement coefficients and wanting to formally test their difference for statistical significance. The extent of agreement among raters could be measured on two occasions. On the first occasion for example, agreement would be measured before the raters receive a formal training, and be measured again after training. The difference between the before-training and the after-training agreement coefficients tells us something about the effectiveness of the training program. Therefore, this difference provides useful information and must be carefully analyzed.

What is statistical significance? In a nutshell, an observed difference is deemed statistically significant if its magnitude cannot be explained by statistical errors alone. A typical agreement coefficient is based on a random sample of subjects and will therefore carry a sampling or statistical error. Its estimated value will differ from the "true" value by a certain margin. Consequently, a sizeable difference can be observed between 2 agreement coefficients due to statistical errors, when in reality there is no difference between the "true" values. Testing a difference for statistical significance amounts to evaluating the likelihood that the observed difference was caused by statistical errors alone. If this likelihood is "small", then the difference is deemed statistical significant.

5.2.1 *The Problem*

A difference between 2 agreement coefficients is deemed "statistically" significant when its magnitude exceeds the maximum value that statistical errors alone are expected to produce. Therefore, an observed difference between agreement coefficients that appears meaningful (i.e. has practical value) to you, should still be tested for statistical significance to ensure that it was not caused by "statistical noise." Statistical noise is typically quantified by the variance associated with the agreement coefficient. Only a meaningful difference that is also statistically significant can ultimately be useful.

When evaluating the difference of 2 agreement coefficients, 2 scenarios must be considered. The first scenario is one where the 2 agreement coefficients are uncorrelated. In the second scenario, the coefficients are deemed correlated. For all practical purposes, 2 agreement coefficients are deemed correlated if they are based on 2 overlapping rosters of raters, 2 overlapping groups of subjects or a mixture of both. On the other hand, 2 agreement coefficients will be uncorrelated if they are based on 2 independent groups of subjects and 2 independent rosters of raters.

Testing uncorrelated agreement coefficients for statistical significance does not pose any problem in particular and relies on standard and well-documented statistical procedures. I will not discuss this scenario in this book. However, interested readers may get more information on these procedures in Gwet (2021b, chap 9-section 9.3.2). But, you should be able to implement all of these procedures in **SAS** using the **SAS/IML** libraries discussed in the past few chapters.

Testing the difference of correlated coefficients is an entirely different problem, the solution of which is briefly reviewed in section 5.2.2. The techniques used to address this problem were initially introduced by Gwet (2016), and further expanded in Gwet (2021b).

5.2.2 The Solution

The general procedure for testing the difference $\widehat{\kappa}_2 - \widehat{\kappa}_1$ between 2 chance-corrected agreement coefficients, consists of first computing the associated standardized difference T (also known as the *Pivot* in statistical jargon) defined by,

$$T = \left(\widehat{\kappa}_2 - \widehat{\kappa}_1\right) / \sqrt{V\left(\widehat{\kappa}_2 - \widehat{\kappa}_1\right)}. \tag{5.2.1}$$

If the pivot's absolute value exceeds a certain threshold then you can conclude that the difference is statistically significant. The challenge of equation 5.2.1 is the computation of the denominator. How do you evaluate the variance of the difference? For uncorrelated coefficients, the variance of the difference equals the sum of individual variances. For correlated coefficients, things may not be trivial. The approach used in this section is that of Gwet (2016), which is based on the "linearization" method . Interested readers may get all the technical details pertaining to this method in Gwet (2021b). In the next paragraph however, I will give you a general flavour of what this technique is about, before presenting the **SAS** program that implements it.

The typical agreement coefficient is a twisting function of individual subject ratings, making it near impossible to untangle the correlation structure of 2 correlated agreement coefficients. However, as the number of subjects increases, the agreement coefficient gets closer to the "true" value it approximates, and becomes more stable around that value. It can be shown mathematically that once an agreement coefficient reaches the vicinity of its "true" value, it can reliably be expressed as a linear function of individual subject-level values. Using this linear expression as a surrogate for the agreement coefficient to calculate the variance of the difference between two coefficients is the technique that underlies the linearization method proposed by Gwet (2016).

Program 5.1 shows how you can use the SAS/IML library of function modules `pairedttest.sas` for testing the difference of 2 agreement coefficients for statistical significance. This library is not used alone. It must be used along with the `weights.sas` library, which I already discussed in previous chapters. These 2 SAS/IML libraries can be downloaded using the following 2 links:

https://agreestat.com/books/sas2/chap5/pairedttest.sas
https://agreestat.com/books/sas2/weights.sas

The segment of Program 5.1 defined by lines **#01** through **#39** reads the 2 datasets used to produce the 2 agreement coefficients being compared. Although both datasets have the same number of raters, this is not a requirement. However, the number of subjects is expected to be same. If not, then only subjects rated by both groups of raters would be used in the paired test. Subjects rated by only one group of raters should be removed. After all, the primary goal for testing the different of 2 correlated is to evaluating the change in rater agreement for a given sample of subjects.

Lines **#43** and **#44** include the two SAS/IML libraries of functions `weights.sas` and `pairedttest.sas` into the program. You will want to change directory names from my directory `c:\kgwet\chap3` to the directory where these libraries are stored. It is in lines **#53** through **#58** that all tests of significance are performed for the 5 agreement coefficients under investigation. Here are the 5 SAS/IML functions that accomplished this task:

- **Fleiss' generalized kappa.** The testing of the difference between 2 correlated Fleiss' kappa coefficients is accomplished with function `ttest_fleiss`, which is defined as follows:

```
start ttest_fleiss(g1_ratings,g2_ratings,
       weights="unweighted",conflev=0.95,Npop=10**7);
```

- **Gwet's AC_2 or AC_1 coefficient.** The testing of the difference between 2 correlated AC_2 (or AC_1) coefficients[1] is done using function `ttest_ac2`. This function is defined as follows:

```
start ttest_ac2(g1_ratings,g2_ratings,
      weights="unweighted",conflev=0.95,Npop=10**7);
```

- **Krippendorff's alpha coefficient.** Function `ttest_alpha` is used for testing the difference between 2 correlated Krippendorff's alpha coefficients, and is defined as follows:

```
start ttest_alpha(g1_ratings,g2_ratings,
      weights="unweighted",conflev=0.95,Npop=10**7);
```

- **Conger's generalized alpha coefficient.** Function `ttest_conger` is used for testing the difference between 2 correlated Conger's generalized kappa coefficients[2], and is defined as follows:

```
start ttest_conger(g1_ratings,g2_ratings,
      weights="unweighted",conflev=0.95,Npop=10**7);
```

- **Brennan-Prediger coefficient.** Function `ttest_bp` is used for testing the difference between 2 correlated Brennan-Prediger coefficients, and is defined as follows:

```
start ttest_bp(g1_ratings,g2_ratings,
      weights="unweighted",conflev=0.95,Npop=10**7);
```

---

[1] Note that AC_1 can be seen as AC_2 based on the set of identity weights.

[2] Remember that Conger's generalized kappa reduces to Cohen's kappa when the number of raters is 2.

All these functions take the same input parameters. `g1_ratings` and `g2_ratings` are the 2 input datasets that will produce the 2 agreement coefficients whose difference will be tested for statistical significance. These are the only 2 mandatory input parameters, the remaining being optional.

`weights` is an optional parameter that defines the set of weights that will be used for computing the agreement coefficient. Its default value is "unweighted". That is, the unweighted analysis will be performed by default. The other possible values this parameter can take are "quadratic", "ordinal", "linear", "radical", "ratio", "circular", and "bipolar". Any character-type value other than those mentioned will be replaced with "unweighted". Section 2.4.3 of chapter 2 describes the different sets of weights that are associated with these names. However, you can also supply a square matrix to this parameter, if you want to use a custom set of weights.

Each of these **SAS/IML** functions returns a list of 2 vectors. The first vector contains the statistics shown in one row of the output table (see Figure 5.1). The second contains the labels associated with the first vector's elements. You may carefully review Program 5.1 to see how it creates the output table.

Program 5.1. SAS program for testing the difference between two agreement coefficients for statistical significance (*You may download this program using the following link:* https://agreestat.com/books/sas2/chap3/prg5pttest.sas)

```
01      proc datasets library=WORK kill; run; quit;
02      data ratings1;
03          input RaterA RaterB RaterC RaterD;
04          datalines;
05      1   1   1   1
06      1   1   2   3
07      1   1   2   3
08      2   2   2   3
09      1   2   1   1
10      2   1   1   1
11      2   2   2   2
12      2   3   2   2
```

```
13      3   3   3   3
14      1   1   1   1
15      1   1   2   3
16      3   3   3   3
17      3   2   3   3
18      1   2   1   1
19      2   1   1   1
20      ;
21  data ratings2;
22          input RaterA RaterB RaterC RaterD;
23          datalines;
24      1   1   1   1
25      3   3   3   2
26      3   3   3   3
27      1   1   2   1
28      1   1   1   1
29      1   1   1   1
30      2   2   2   2
31      2   2   1   1
32      3   3   3   3
33      1   1   1   3
34      2   2   2   2
35      3   3   3   3
36      3   3   3   3
37      1   2   1   1
38      3   3   3   3
39      ;
40  ods pdf file="c:\kgwet\chap5\pairedttest.pdf" style=Ocean;
41  title "Paired t-test for testing 2 correlated coefficients";
42  proc iml;
43      %inc "C:\kgwet\chap5\weights.sas";
44      %inc "C:\kgwet\chap5\pairedttest.sas";
45      use ratings1;
46          read all var _NUM_ into mratings1[colname=rNames];
47      close ratings1;
48      use ratings2;
49          read all var _NUM_ into mratings2[colname=rNames];
50      close ratings2;
51      print mratings1 " " mratings2;
53      fl_outlst = ttest_fleiss(mratings1,mratings2);
55      cg_outlst = ttest_conger(mratings1,mratings2);
56      ac_outlst = ttest_ac2(mratings1,mratings2);
57      bp_outlst = ttest_bp(mratings1,mratings2);
```

```
58          kr_outlst = ttest_alpha(mratings1,mratings2);
59          out = shape(0,5,6);
60          out[1,] = t(round(fl_outlst$1,1/10**4));
61          out[2,] = t(round(cg_outlst$1,1/10**4));
62          out[3,] = t(round(ac_outlst$1,1/10**4));
63          out[4,] = t(round(bp_outlst$1,1/10**4));
64          out[5,] = t(round(kr_outlst$1,1/10**4));
65
66          cnames = {"Coeff1","Coeff2","Diff","S.E.(Diff)",
67                      "t-Stat","P-Value"};
68          rnames = putc(repeat("",5), "$20.");
69          rnames[1] = substr(fl_outlst$2[1],1,
70                      length(fl_outlst$2[1])-1);
71          rnames[2] = substr(cg_outlst$2[1],1,
72                      length(cg_outlst$2[1])-1);
73          rnames[3] = substr(ac_outlst$2[1],1,
74                      length(ac_outlst$2[1])-1);
75          rnames[4] = substr(bp_outlst$2[1],1,
76                      length(bp_outlst$2[1])-1);
77          rnames[5] = substr(kr_outlst$2[1],1,
78                      length(kr_outlst$2[1])-1);
79
80          mattrib out r=rnames c=cnames;
81          print out[label=""];
82      quit;
83      ods pdf close;
```

	Coeff1	Coeff2	Diff	S.E.(Diff)	t-Stat	P-Value
Fleiss Kappa	0.3857	0.7248	0.3392	0.1574	2.1545	0.0491
Conger Kappa	0.3933	0.7251	0.3318	0.1527	2.1728	0.0475
AC1/2 Coeff	0.4069	0.7374	0.3305	0.1453	2.2748	0.0392
BP Coeff	0.4	0.7333	0.3333	0.1477	2.2563	0.0406
Krippendorff Alpha	0.3959	0.7294	0.3335	0.1548	2.1545	0.0491

Figure 5.1: Hypothesis testing of the difference between 2 correlated agreement coefficients for statistical significance. Output produced by Program 5.1.

5.3   Benchmarking Agreement Coefficients

Benchmarking is essential for communicating the results of a reliability study to a wide audience, in addition to providing guidelines that help practitioners with the use of agreement statistics. Quantifying the extent of agreement is one thing. However, knowing whether the magnitude of the agreement coefficient is good or not is another important problem that cannot be overlooked. Benchmarking allows you to match the magnitude of a given agreement coefficient to known standards so it can be qualified as poor or good or anything else in between.

5.3.1   *Benchmarking Models*

Three benchmarking models proposed in the literature are reviewed in this section. Although these models were developed to be used primarily with the kappa coefficient, they are often used in practice with other agreement coefficients as well. Table 5.1 describes the benchmark scale that Landis and Koch (1977) proposed. It follows from this table that the extent of agreement can be qualified as "Poor", "Slight", "Fair", "Moderate", "Substantial" and "Almost Perfect" depending on the magnitude of Kappa. A Kappa value between 40% and 60% for example indicates a moderate agreement level, while ranges of values (60% – 80%), and (80% – 100%) indicate substantial and almost perfect agreement levels respectively. Although the authors acknowledge the subjective nature of their benchmarks, they recommended them as a useful guideline for practitioners. Other authors such as Everitt (1992) have supported this benchmark scale.

Fleiss (1981) proposed another benchmark scale where the first three value ranges of the Landis-Koch benchmark are collapsed into a single range "0.40 or less" labeled as "Poor." Table 5.2 shows the 3 ranges of values that make up

Fleiss' benchmarking scale. Kappa values in the 40% − 75% range for example represent an "Intermediate to Good" extent of agreement, while all Kappa values in the 75% − 100% range indicate an "Excellent" extent of agreement. This scale has the advantage of having a small number of categories while presenting the middle category as that of acceptable values, the low-end category as that of the unacceptable, and the high-end category as that of excellence.

Table 5.1: Landis and Koch Kappa's Benchmark Scale[a]

Kappa Statistic	Strength of Agreement
−1.0 to 0.0	Poor
0.0 to 0.20	Slight
0.20 to 0.40	Fair
0.40 to 0.60	Moderate
0.60 to 0.80	Substantial
0.80 to 1.00	Almost Perfect

[a]Note that in the original Landis-Koch scale, the first interval is defined as "< 0", while the lower bounds of the remaining intervals are 0.0, 0.21, 0.41, 0.61, and 0.81. The proposed changes are motivated by the fact that most agreement coefficients take values on a continuum between -1 and 1. The original intervals leave out some values that are part of this continuum.

Table 5.2: Fleiss' Kappa Benchmark Scale

Kappa Statistic	Strength of Agreement
< 0.40	Poor
0.40 to 0.75	Intermediate to Good
More than 0.75	Excellent

Altman (1991) proposed another benchmark scale summarized in Table 5.3, and which represents a modified version of the Landis-Koch's proposal. The only noticeable difference is that the first two ranges of values in Landis-Koch's proposal are collapsed into a single category labeled as "Poor" in Altman's scale. Landis-Koch's proposed benchmarking method was published several years before Alman's, and is still being used today. Therefore, the argument for supporting the newer Altman's benchmarks remains unclear.

Table 5.3: Altman's Kappa Benchmark Scale[a]

Kappa Statistic	Strength of Agreement
-1.0 to 0.20	Poor
0.20 to 0.40	Fair
0.40 to 0.60	Moderate
0.60 to 0.80	Good
0.80 to 1.00	Very Good

[a]Note that in the original Altman scale, the first interval is defined as "< 0.20", while the lower bounds of the remaining intervals are 0.21, 0.41, 0.61, and 0.81. The proposed changes are motivated by the fact that most agreement coefficients take values on a continuum between -1 and 1. The original intervals leave out some values that are included in that continuum.

5.3.2   *Using the Benchmark Scales*

I do not recommend matching an agreement coefficient estimate to an existing benchmark scale to qualify its magnitude. Although many researchers have done it, this approach has a major problem. Consider for example the Landis-Koch benchmark scale of Table 5.1 and an agreement coefficient estimate of 0.42. If you match this estimate with standards of Table 5.1, you will qualify the extent of agreement among raters as "Moderate". However, if the confidence interval associated with this coefficient covers the 0.20-0.40 range of values for example, then the "true" agreement coefficient may well be qualified as "fair." Why would you want to claim the agreement level to be "Moderate" based on a rough estimate, when the error-free estimand could lead to a different conclusion?

> *Therefore, the error margin should be an integral part of any benchmarking strategy for it to be methodologically sound.*

Note that a larger number of subjects will generally lead to a more precise agreement coefficient, which is expected to be close to the true value it approximates. Therefore, matching a precise coefficient with existing benchmarks will lead to conclusions that apply to some extent to the true parameter of interest as well. A small number of subjects on the other hand, reduces the precision of the inter-rater reliability coefficient, in addition to exposing that precision to further degradation due possibly to a small number of raters, or a small number of response categories. Taking an agreement coefficient, which is subject to a substantial statistical error and matching it to a predetermined quality benchmark can only produce a questionable characterization of the extent of agreement among raters.

The recommended benchmarking method is a three-step procedure:

(i) The first step consists of quantifying for any given agreement coefficient and benchmark scale of choice, the probability that the extent of agreement falls into each of the intervals defining the benchmark levels. For each interval, a membership probability will be calculated. A more mathematical description of the membership probability is provided by Gwet (2021a, chap. 7).

(ii) As a second step, you would compute the interval cumulative probabilities starting from the high end interval[3] and going down to the low end. That is, the cumulative probability associated with the top interval is identical to the probability calculated in step (i) for that interval. For the second interval in descending order, the cumulative probability is obtained by summing the membership probabilities of the two top intervals.

---

[3]The top interval is the range of values in the benchmark scale containing the highest values.

(*iii*) *The final benchmark level is determined by the interval associated with the smallest cumulative probability that exceeds 95%.* You will then be in a position to conclude with 95% certainty or more that the extent of agreement among raters is for example "Excellent." This approach allows for a fair comparison between different studies using the same agreement statistic even though they are based on different designs.

To see how this process works, look at the 2 Figures 5.2 and 5.3. The third column of Figure 5.3's table is labeled as "`pa_cprob`" and contains the cumulative membership probabilities (CMP) associated with the percent agreement p_a. For example, 0.5222484 represents the probability that the "true" percent agreement belong to interval $(0.8; 1)$. However, 0.9555181 is the probability that the "true" percent agreement exceeds 0.6 (i.e. it belongs either to interval 0.8-1 or to interval 0.6-0.8). As you move down that third column, the probabilities will cumulate until the last row when it reaches its maximum value of 1. Since interval $(0.6; 0.8)$ is the first one (from the top down) with a CMP that exceeds 0.95, the associated interpretation as "Good" will be reported for the percent agreement.

The remaining columns in Figure 5.3 table are labeled as "`ac_cprob`", "`fl_cprob`" and "`kr_cprob`" and contain CMP values for Gwet's AC_1, Fleiss kappa and Krippendorff's alpha coefficients. It follows from these numbers that all 3 agreement coefficients are interpreted as "Moderate". You should not just look at Figure 5.2 table coefficients estimated above 0.74 and conclude that they should be interpreted as "Good" since they fall into interval (0.6-0.8). The interpretation of these coefficients is demoted to "Moderate" due to their standard errors that are high because the analysis is based on a small sample of only 12 subjects.

In Program 5.2, lines #22, #23 and #24 include the 3 SAS/IML libraries `weights`, `agreecoeff3raw.sas` and `benchmarking.sas`. The new SAS/IML library `benchmarking.sas` contains one main function, which is defined as follows:

```
start bench_cumprob(coeff,se,bench_mat);
```

This is the function that computes the Cumulative Membership Probabilities (CMP) of Figure 5.3's table. It is called 5 times in lines #50 through #59 to compute CMP estimates for the percent agreement, Gwet's AC_1, Fleiss' kappa, Brennan-Prediger and Krippendorff's alpha.

Program 5.2. SAS program for computing cumulative membership probabilities to benchmark agreement coefficients (*To download this program, follow the link:* https://agreestat.com/books/sas2/chap3/prg5benchmark.sas)

```
01   proc datasets library=WORK kill; run; quit;
02   data ratings;
03     input r1-r4;
04     datalines;
05   1 1 . 1
06   2 2 3 2
07   3 3 3 3
08   3 3 3 3
09   2 2 2 2
10   1 2 3 4
11   4 4 4 4
12   1 1 2 1
13   2 2 2 2
14   . 5 5 5
15   . . 1 1
16   . . 3 .
17   ;
18
19   ods pdf file="c:\kgwet\chap5\benchmark.pdf" style=Ocean;
20     proc print data=ratings;run;
21     proc iml;
22       %inc "c:\kgwet\chap5\weights.sas";
23       %inc "c:\kgwet\chap5\agreecoeff3raw.sas";
24       %inc "c:\kgwet\chap5\benchmarking.sas";
25       use ratings;
26         read all var _NUM_ into mratings[colname=rNames];
27       close ratings;
28
29         pa_outlst = pa_coeff_raw(mratings);
```

```
30      cg_outlst = conger_kappa_raw(mratings);
31      fl_outlst = fleiss_kappa_raw(mratings);
32      ac_outlst = gwet_ac1_raw(mratings);
33      bp_outlst = bp_coeff_raw(mratings);
34      kr_outlst = krippen_alpha_raw(mratings);
35
36      out = shape(0,6,5);
37      out[1,] = t(pa_outlst$1);out[2,] = t(cg_outlst$1);
38      out[3,] = t(fl_outlst$1);out[4,] = t(ac_outlst$1);
39      out[5,] = t(bp_outlst$1);out[6,] = t(kr_outlst$1);
40
41      cnames = {"Coeff","Std Err","LCB","UCB","P-Value"};
42      rnames = putc(repeat("",6), "$20.");
43      rnames[1] = pa_outlst$2[1];rnames[2] = cg_outlst$2[1];
44      rnames[3] = fl_outlst$2[1];rnames[4] = ac_outlst$2[1];
45      rnames[5] = bp_outlst$2[1];rnames[6] = kr_outlst$2[1];
46
47      mattrib out r=rnames c=cnames;
48      print out[label=""];
49
50      pa_cprob = bench_cumprob(pa_outlst$1[1],
51                              pa_outlst$1[2],alt_mat);
52      ac_cprob = bench_cumprob(ac_outlst$1[1],
53                              ac_outlst$1[2],alt_mat);
54      fl_cprob = bench_cumprob(fl_outlst$1[1],
55                              fl_outlst$1[2],alt_mat);
56      bp_cprob = bench_cumprob(bp_outlst$1[1],
57                              bp_outlst$1[2],alt_mat);
58      kr_cprob = bench_cumprob(kr_outlst$1[1],
59                              kr_outlst$1[2],alt_mat);
60
61      nitems = nrow(pa_cprob);
62      altRange=putc(repeat("",nitems,1),"$10.");
63      do i=1 to nitems;
64        altRange[i] = strip(char(alt_mat[i,1])) +
65                      " to " + strip(char(alt_mat[i,2]));
66      end;
67      print altRange[L="Alt Range"] alt_interp
68      pa_cprob ac_cprob fl_cprob kr_cprob;
69    quit;
70  ods pdf close;
```

	Coeff	Std Err	LCB	UCB	P-Value
Percent Agreement	0.8181818	0.12561	0.54172	1	0.0000435
Conger's Kappa	0.76282	0.14917	0.4345	1	0.0003367
Fleiss Kappa	0.7611693	0.15302	0.42438	1	0.0004192
Gwet AC1/AC2	0.7754441	0.14295	0.46081	1	0.0002087
BP Coefficient	0.7727273	0.14472	0.45421	1	0.0002376
Krippendorff Alpha	0.7434211	0.14548	0.42322	1	0.0003386

Figure 5.2: Agreement coefficients calculated with Program 5.2

Alt Range	alt_interp	pa_cprob	ac_cprob	fl_cprob	kr_cprob
0.8 to 1	Very Good	0.5222484	0.3967528	0.3620149	0.3223128
0.6 to 0.8	Good	0.9555181	0.8833701	0.8446796	0.831336
0.4 to 0.6	Moderate	0.9995298	0.9954192	0.9902938	0.9905083
0.2 to 0.4	Fair	0.9999995	0.9999698	0.9998697	0.9999025
-1 to 0.2	Poor	1	1	1	1

Figure 5.3: Cumulative membership probabilities calculated produced by Program 5.2

Bibliography

Altman, D.G. (1991), *Practical Statistics for Medical Research*. Chapman and Hall.

Banerjee, M., M. Capozzoli, L. McSweeney, and D. Sinha (1999), "Beyond kappa: A review of interrater agreement measures." *Thr Canadian Journal of Statistics*, 27, 3–23.

Brennan, R.L. and D.J. Prediger (1981), "Coefficient kappa: some uses, misuses, and alternatives." *Educational and Psychological Measurement*, 41, 687–699.

Byrt, T., J. Bishop, and J.B. Carlin (1993), "Bias, prevalence and kappa." *Journal of Clinical Epidemiology*, 46, 423–429.

Cicchetti, D.V. and T. Allison (1971), "A new procedure for assessing reliability of scoring eeg sleep recording." *American Journal of EEG Technology*, 11, 101–109.

Cicchetti, D.V. and A.R. Feinstein (1990), "High agreement but low kappa: Ii. resolving the paradoxes." *Journal of Clinical Epidemiology*, 43, 551–558.

Cohen, J. (1960), "A coefficient of agreement for nominal scales." *Educational and Psychological Measurement*, 20, 37–46.

Cohen, J. (1968), "Weighted kappa: Nominal scale agreement with provision for scaled disagreement or partial credit." *Psychological Bulletin*, 70, 213–220.

Conger, A.J. (1980), "Integration and generalization of kappas for multiple raters." *Psychological Bulletin*, 88, 322–328.

Crewson, P.E. (2001), "A correction for unbalanced kappa tables." http://www2.sas.com/proceedings/sugi26/p194-26.pdf.

Everitt, B.S. (1992), *The Analysis of Contingency Tables*, 2 edition. Chapman and Hall, London.

Feinstein, A.R. and D.V. Cicchetti (1990), "High agreement but low kappa: I. the problems of two paradoxes." *Journal of Clinical Epidemiology*, 43, 543–549.

Finn, R.H. (1970), "A note on estimating the reliability of categorical data." *Educational and Psychological Measurement*, 30, 71–76.

Fleiss, J.L. (1971), "Measuring nominal scale agreement among many raters." *Psychological Bulletin*, 76, 378–382.

Fleiss, J.L. (1981), *Statistical Methods for Rates and Proportions*. John Wiley & Sons.

Fleiss, J.L. and J. Cohen (1973), "The equivalence of weighted kappa and the intraclass correlation coefficient as measures of reliability." *Educational and Psychological Measurement*, 33, 613–619.

Fleiss, J.L., B. Levin, and M.C. Paik (2003), *Statistical Methods for Rates and Proportions*, 3 edition. Wiley Series in Probability and Statistics, Wiley-Interscience.

Gwet, Kilem L. (2008a), "Computing inter-rater reliability and its variance in the presence of high agreement." *British Journal of Mathematical and Statistical Psychology*, 61, 29–48.

Gwet, Kilem L. (2016), "Testing the difference of correlated agreement coefficients for statistical significance." *Educational and Psychological Measurement*, 76, 609–637.

Gwet, Kilem L. (2021a), *Handbook of Inter-Rater Reliability - Volume 1: Chance-corrected Agreement Coefficients for Categorical Ratings*, 5 edition, volume 1. AgreeStat Analytics, Maryland, USA.

Gwet, Kilem L. (2021b), *Handbook of Inter-Rater Reliability - Volume 2: Intraclass Correlation Coefficients for Quantitative Ratings*, 5 edition, volume 1. AgreeStat Analytics, Maryland, USA.

Gwet, K.L. (2021c), "Large-sample variance of fleiss generalized kappa." *Educational and Psychological Measurement*, 81, 781–790.

Krippendorff, K. (1970), "Estimating the reliability, systematic error, and random error of interval data." *Educational and Psychological Measurement*, 30, 61–70.

Krippendorff, K. (1978), "Reliability of binary attribute data." *Biometrics*, 34, 142–144.

Krippendorff, Klaus (2004), "Measuring the reliability of qualitative text analysis data." *Quality and Quantity*, 38, 787–800.

Landis, J.R. and G. Koch (1977), "The measurement of observer agreement for categorical data." *Biometrics*, 33, 159–174.

Light, R.J. (1971), "Measures of response agreement for qualitative data: some generalizations and alternatives." *Psychological Bulletin*, 76, 365–377.

Liu, H. and R.D. Hays (1999), *Measurement of Interrater Agreement: A SAS/IML Macro Kappa Procedure for Handling Incomplete Data*, 1620–1625. -.

Scott, W.A. (1955), "Reliability of content analysis: the case of nominal scale coding." *Public Opinion Quarterly*, XIX, 321–325.

Shrout, P.E. and J.L. Fleiss (1979), "Intraclass correlations: Uses in assessing rater reliability." *Psychological Bulletin*, 86, 420–428.

Siegel, S. and N.J. Castellan Jr. (1988), *Nonparametric Statistics for the Behavioral Sciences*, 2 edition. McGraw-Hill Book Company, New York.

Stein, C.R., R.B. Devore Jr., and B.E. Wojcik (2005), "Calculation of the kappa statistic for inter-rater reliability: The case where raters can select multiple responses from a large number of categories." In *Proceedings of the Thirtieth Annual SAS Users Group International Conference*, SAS Users Group.

List of Notations

Author Index

Subject Index

For updates and more resources, use the following link:

https://agreestat.com/books/sas2/

www.ingramcontent.com/pod-product-compliance
Lightning Source LLC
Chambersburg PA
CBHW081951260726
48657CB00009BA/2558